Chapter 1: The Journey Begins

Sophie is a sixteen-year-old girl who feels like the weight of the world is resting on her shoulders. Every morning, she wakes up early to prepare for another day of school, and with each passing day, the pressure grows. Her schoolwork keeps piling up, and her friendships seem more complicated than they used to be. It feels like everyone around her has it all figured out, yet she finds herself lost in a sea of thoughts and emotions that she can't quite grasp. Despite her bright smile and friendly demeanor, there is a growing sense of unease bubbling within her. She has a nagging feeling that something isn't right, but she struggles to put her finger on what it is or how to talk about it with anyone.

At school, Sophie tries to keep up with her classes. She makes sure to take thorough notes, study hard for tests, and participate in group discussions. Yet, despite her efforts, she often feels anxious when she's sitting in class. The math problems seem harder, the reading assignments feel longer, and the pressure to perform well weighs heavily on her mind. Her teachers often praise her for her hard work, yet Sophie can't shake the feeling that she is barely keeping her head above water. Sometimes, during lunch, she glances around the cafeteria at her classmates. They seem to be enjoying themselves, laughing and chatting freely. Sophie wants to join in on the fun, but she feels a barrier between herself and the carefree spirit of her peers.

Sophie's friendships are also a source of confusion for her. She used to be close with a group of girls, sharing secrets and laughter. However, as they have grown older, it seems that they have grown apart. They now have different interests, and Sophie feels like she doesn't fit in as well as she used to. This change is disheartening for her. She often finds herself scrolling through social media, watching her friends share pictures and stories that leave her feeling like an outsider. The anxiety of possibly reaching out and inviting them for a hangout weighs heavily. What if they don't want to spend time with her anymore? What if she is the only one who feels this way?

One evening, Sophie sits on her bed, looking through her journals. Writing has always been a way for her to organize her thoughts. The pages are filled with her thoughts, dreams, fears, and hopes.

She often writes about how she wishes her friendships were like they were before. She pens down her longing for days spent laughing with her friends over silly things. As she reads back, she admires the way she could easily express herself in the written word, yet she struggles to articulate her feelings verbally. This realization strikes her, making her wonder how many others share the same silent struggle within.

On her nightstand, there sits a book that caught her attention a few days ago. It's about discovering oneself in a chaotic world. Sophie picks it up and starts to read. The pages encourage readers to take small steps toward self-discovery and emotional awareness. She finds the ideas engaging, and with each turn of the page, she feels a sense of inspiration growing inside her. It provides simple techniques for grounding oneself when feelings of anxiety arise, such as taking deep breaths, going for short walks, or even engaging in creative outlets. As Sophie contemplates these tips, she realizes that she can make small changes in her life that might help her navigate her emotions better.

The next day, armed with this newfound insight, Sophie decides to take a walk after school. She often rushes home right after classes, but today feels different. With each step down the bustling street, she focuses on her surroundings. She notices the sound of laughter from children playing in a nearby park, the colors of the flowers lining the sidewalks, and the gentle rustle of leaves in the breeze. This brief moment of mindfulness brings her an unexpected sense of peace. It feels nice to disconnect from the digital noise of her social media and just be in the moment.

Later that week, Sophie tries another suggestion from the book. She sets aside a few minutes each day to draw or sketch. Drawing has never been her strongest suit, but there is something liberating about expressing herself on paper without the fear of judgment. She begins to create simple images of the things that make her happy: her dog playing in the yard, the colorful flowers in her mother's garden, and even small, whimsical creatures inspired by her imagination. Each sketch becomes an outlet for her feelings, allowing her to explore her inner world in a way that she hasn't done before.

While new hobbies and gentle walks help ease some of her worries, Sophie still feels a lingering desire for connection. She decides it's time to reach out to her friends, even if it feels daunting. The thought of sending a simple text takes her several days, as she continuously drafts and revises her message in her mind. Finally, she types out a message inviting them to a local coffee shop for a catch-up. With a deep breath, she hits send and immediately feels a rush of anxiety. She wonders if they will respond positively or leave her hanging.

To her surprise, a few hours later, she receives replies that light up her screen. Her friends are excited and suggest meeting up that weekend. This small exchange brings a glimmer of hope to Sophie. She realizes that taking the step to reach out was a significant moment in her journey. Each friendly response feels like a thread pulling her back into the fabric of friendship, stitching together the spaces that felt torn apart.

As the weekend approaches, Sophie feels both anxious and excited. The thought of reconnecting with her friends fills her with anticipation. She prepares herself for their gathering, choosing a casual outfit that makes her feel comfortable yet confident. When the day arrives, she arrives at the coffee shop early, feeling the butterflies of both nervousness and eagerness. Each passing minute feels like an eternity until her friends walk through the door, laughter spilling into the cozy space.

The moment they sit down together, Sophie realizes that things may not be exactly how they were before, but that is okay. They share stories, reminisce about childhood days, and discuss their current lives. Sophie notices the familiarity and warmth between them, a feeling she missed dearly. It's as if the threads of friendship had never truly unraveled; they merely needed a little reminder of what made them close in the first place.

Through this experience, Sophie learns about the importance of communication and vulnerability. While her journey is still ongoing, she begins to understand that feeling overwhelmed is a part of life. She realizes that taking small steps, being honest with herself and others, can ease some of her burdens. This chapter of her life is just beginning, and with it comes the promise of growth, connection, and self-discovery.

Chapter 2: What is Mental Health?

Sophie is a young girl who is starting to understand the importance of taking care of her mind. One day, she sits down with her parents and her teacher to have a chat about mental health. They explain to her that mental health is about how we think, feel, and act. Just like taking care of our bodies is essential for our physical health, looking after our mental well-being is equally important. This discussion opens up a window for Sophie to see how her thoughts and feelings influence her everyday life.

Her parents begin by sharing what mental health means. They tell her that it involves more than just the absence of mental illness. Mental health includes emotional, psychological, and social well-being. For example, when Sophie feels happy or excited, she experiences good mental health. However, when she feels sad or anxious, her mental health may take a hit. This explanation helps Sophie realize that her emotions are valid and not something to shy away from.

Sophie's teacher then joins the conversation and emphasizes how important it is to maintain good mental health, just like we maintain physical health. Her teacher explains that regular exercise, eating well, and getting enough sleep help keep our bodies healthy. Similarly, there are things we can do to care for our minds. The teacher provides simple steps to improve mental health. For instance, practicing mindfulness can help Sophie feel more present and less overwhelmed. Mindfulness involves paying attention to the moment, allowing us to understand our emotions better.

Her teacher also discusses the importance of talking about feelings. Sophie learns that sharing her thoughts and emotions with others can lighten heavy burdens. Her parents agree and encourage her to speak up whenever she's feeling down. They believe that it's okay to ask for help when needed. They share examples from their lives where talking to friends or family made a positive difference. Sophie feels reassured to know that she can reach out to others.

Then, they talk about self-care, which is essential for mental well-being. Self-care means taking time for oneself to relax and recharge. Sophie's dad suggests engaging in hobbies, like painting or playing sports, as a way to express herself and relieve stress. Her mom mentions that reading books or going for walks can also be calming activities. Sophie realizes that self-care does not have to be complicated; it can be as simple as spending time doing things she loves.

As the discussion continues, they touch on the significance of setting goals. Sophie learns that having short-term and long-term goals can provide direction and a sense of purpose. For instance, if Sophie wants to improve in her math class, she can set small, achievable goals, like studying for 30 minutes each day. Her teacher highlights how accomplishing these goals, no matter how small, can boost confidence and improve her mental outlook.

Sophie's parents and teacher then delve into how external factors can impact mental health. They explain how things like school pressures, friendships, or family dynamics can create stress. Sophie's parents share a personal story about a time when they felt stressed due to work obligations. They explain that finding ways to cope, such as talking it out or practicing stress-relief techniques, helped them navigate tough times.

They also discuss the importance of social connections. Her teacher explains that spending time with friends and family is vital for mental health. Whether it's hanging out with friends at school or having family movie nights, these moments of connection can strengthen relationships and improve overall well-being. Sophie realizes that nurturing these connections can bring joy and support when needed.

As the conversation wraps up, Sophie asks how she can recognize when her mental health might be slipping. Her teacher provides essential signs to watch out for, such as persistent sadness, changes in sleep patterns, or withdrawing from friends. Her mom adds that feeling overwhelmed or anxious for extended periods can also be warning signs. Sophie feels grateful for their guidance and knows that being aware of these signs is crucial.

Through their conversation, Sophie gains a deeper understanding of mental health.

She feels empowered to take action in caring for her mind and emotions. Sophie starts to think about her daily routine and how she can incorporate some of the strategies her parents and teacher mentioned. She considers journaling her feelings, doing yoga to calm her mind, and making time for her favorite activities.

Her parents remind her that it's okay to experience ups and downs. They assure her that everyone has moments of doubt or sadness, and these feelings are part of being human. They stress that mental health is a journey and that everyone has their path to navigate. Sophie feels comforted knowing that she doesn't have to be perfect and that seeking help is a strength, not a weakness.

As Sophie reflects on the conversation, she thinks about how she can support her friends too. Maybe she can talk to her classmates about mental health so they also feel comfortable expressing themselves. Her teacher encourages this idea, explaining that by starting conversations and being there for others, Sophie can help create a supportive environment at school.

Ultimately, Sophie leaves the discussion with a stronger sense of awareness and purpose. She recognizes that mental health is multifaceted, involving emotions, relationships, and personal well-being. Armed with this knowledge, Sophie feels ready to tackle her challenges and support those around her. It's a journey, but she knows she has the resources and support to navigate it. Sophie's growth continues as she embraces her feelings and the importance of mental health in her life.

Chapter 3: Understanding Emotions

Sophie begins her journey by exploring the different emotions that people experience in their daily lives. Each emotion plays a significant role and provides valuable insights into how we react to the world around us. Emotions such as happiness, sadness, anger, and fear are not just fleeting feelings; they help illuminate what is happening inside us. For Sophie, understanding these emotions becomes a way to better navigate her experiences.

Firstly, let's take a closer look at happiness. Happiness is often described as a positive emotion that brings joy and satisfaction. Sophie learns that happiness can come from simple things like spending time with friends, enjoying a sunny day, or achieving a goal. For instance, when Sophie plays with her dog in the park, she feels a wave of happiness wash over her. This feeling is not just a moment; it serves as a reminder of what she values and enjoys. Understanding happiness allows Sophie to seek out those moments more intentionally in her life.

Next, Sophie encounters sadness. This emotion can arise from various situations, like losing something important or feeling lonely. Sophie learns that sadness is a natural response to life's challenges. When her friend moves away, Sophie feels sad. Instead of pushing this feeling aside, she recognizes it as an important clue. Sadness teaches Sophie about her connections to others and the importance of cherishing her relationships. To cope with sadness, Sophie tries different strategies, such as talking to her family about her feelings or writing in a journal. By acknowledging her sadness, she finds healthier ways to process her emotions.

Anger is another emotion that Sophie discovers. Anger can sometimes feel overwhelming, but it is a valid emotion that signals when something is wrong or unfair. For example, if someone cuts in front of Sophie in line, she might feel angry. Rather than letting this anger build up, Sophie learns that expressing it in a constructive way is vital. She practices deep breathing and counts to ten to calm herself before responding. Through this process, she learns to communicate her feelings more assertively instead of letting anger dictate her actions. Anger can be helpful when it leads to constructive change.

Fear is an emotion that many people experience, and Sophie is no different. Fear can be protective, alerting us to potential danger, but it can also hold us back from trying new things. Sophie remembers a time when she felt afraid to present her school project in front of the class. This fear made her want to hide, but she learns that facing her fears can lead to personal growth. To prepare for her presentation, Sophie practices in front of a mirror and imagines how her classmates might react. Gradually, she finds that the fear begins to lessen. This experience teaches her that it's okay to feel afraid, but taking small steps to confront that fear can help her overcome it.

Sophie also learns that emotions are not fixed; they can change from moment to moment. For instance, she may start the day feeling happy, but a small incident can trigger feelings of sadness or anger. Recognizing this fluidity helps Sophie understand that emotions are part of being human. She reflects on her emotional ups and downs as she navigates friendship dynamics at school. One moment, she might feel excited about a playdate, and the next, she might envy a friend's attention. By acknowledging these shifting emotions, Sophie becomes more aware of her feelings and why they change.

Understanding emotions also involves recognizing that they can influence each other. Joy can transform into sadness when mixed with nostalgia, while fear can turn into anger when we feel trapped. Sophie notices how her emotions intertwine during different experiences. For example, during a family outing, she feels happy when everyone is laughing together. But later, when she sees an old photo reminding her of a beloved pet that has passed away, sadness washes over her. By seeing and accepting these connections, she learns the importance of full emotional awareness.

Sophie discovers practical ways to manage her emotions effectively. She starts to create a list of things that make her feel good. This list includes activities like drawing, going for walks, or listening to her favorite music. When she feels a strong emotion, Sophie refers to this list as a helpful tool. Having a go-to list empowers her to take action rather than feeling overwhelmed.

Another approach Sophie learns is mindfulness. Mindfulness means being present and aware of what's happening in the moment. During moments of intense emotion, she tries to take deep breaths and notice her feelings without judgment. This technique helps her step back and observe her emotions from a distance. By doing this, she realizes that while feelings are important, they do not have to control her actions. This practice becomes a significant part of how she manages her emotional landscape.

Sophie's journey also involves understanding how different factors can influence her emotions. She learns about the impact of her surroundings, such as the people she is with or the places she frequents. For example, she feels energized and happy whenever she is at her favorite park, surrounded by nature. In contrast, she might feel anxious in crowded places. By recognizing these influences, Sophie understands that she can make choices about where to spend her time to create a more positive emotional environment.

Sophie's friends also contribute to her understanding of emotions. She learns that sharing feelings can be a bonding experience. Through conversations with her close friends, she discovers that they also experience a wide range of emotions. They share their own stories of happiness, sadness, anger, and fear, creating a safe space for everyone to learn from each other. Together, they support one another through ups and downs, reinforcing the idea that no one is alone in their emotions.

As Sophie navigates her emotional journey, she realizes that seeking help is a sign of strength. She starts talking to an adult she trusts when she feels overwhelmed. This person helps her process her feelings more deeply. Seeking help feels empowering and reassures her that it's okay to lean on others during tough times. This realization marks a significant growth point for Sophie and enriches her understanding of her feelings.

In addition to emotional support from others, Sophie also comes to value the importance of self-care. She learns about various self-care strategies to nurture her emotional well-being. Simple actions like taking a warm bath, drawing, or enjoying a favorite snack can help calm her mind. By incorporating these self-care practices into her daily routine, she begins to feel more in control of her emotions.

Through her exploration, Sophie becomes more compassionate towards herself. She learns that experiencing a range of emotions is part of the human experience. It is okay to be happy one moment and sad the next. Emotions are valid, and it's essential to acknowledge them without guilt or shame. By treating herself with kindness, Sophie cultivates a healthier relationship with her feelings.

Sophie's understanding of emotions deepens as she reflects on her experiences. She discovers a new level of emotional literacy, which empowers her to express herself more clearly. Writing in her journal becomes a powerful tool for reflection. Not only can she capture her feelings on paper, but she also learns to identify patterns in her emotional responses. This practice helps her better prepare for and manage future emotional challenges.

Chapter 4: Talking About Feelings

Sophie found it very difficult to express her feelings. At school, she would often keep her emotions to herself. She noticed that the other kids around her seemed to share their thoughts easily. They laughed, expressed joy, and even shared their worries about homework and grades. But for Sophie, it was not so simple. Whenever she tried to talk about her feelings, her words felt stuck. She often thought about why it was hard to express herself. The words would swirl in her mind, but getting them out was another challenge.

One day, Sophie's teacher, noticing her struggle, suggested she talk to the school counselor. The thought of meeting with someone she didn't know made her nervous. What would she say? Would the counselor think she was silly for not being able to talk about her feelings? However, Sophie gathered her courage and decided to go. Meeting the counselor turned out to be a positive experience. The counselor was warm and easy to talk to. They began by discussing daily events, then slowly moved into deeper topics.

The counselor explained that everyone has emotions and that it is perfectly normal to feel overwhelmed at times. She encouraged Sophie to think about her feelings as if they were colors. Some days, she might feel bright and colorful, while other days could feel gray or dull. This simple analogy helped Sophie relate to her feelings in a tangible way. The counselor then introduced her to some methods for expressing feelings, such as journaling, drawing, or even talking to a trusted friend. Sophie decided to give journaling a try. She bought a special notebook and began writing about her day, her thoughts, and her emotions.

As time went on, Sophie realized that writing helped her understand herself better. When she would sit down to write, she found that the words began to flow. She learned to identify her feelings, like sadness, anger, or joy, and give them names. For example, one day she wrote, "Today, I felt really sad when I saw my friend playing with someone else." By putting her feelings on paper, she felt a sense of relief. It was as if she was letting a little bit of the weight off her shoulders.

After feeling more confident about expressing her emotions on paper, Sophie was ready to share some of her thoughts with her friends. One Friday, while hanging out at the park, she decided it was time to have a heart-to-heart conversation. She took a deep breath and said, "Hey, can we talk about how we feel sometimes?" Her friends looked at her curiously. Sophie felt a flutter of nerves in her stomach, but she pushed through.

To her surprise, her friends were receptive. One of her friends, Emma, spoke up, "I often feel left out when you guys hang out without me." This opened the door for everyone to share. Tom admitted he felt stressed about school and homework. As the conversation flowed, more feelings were uncovered. Laughter mixed with tears as they shared their worries and joys. Sophie realized that talking about feelings was not just about the heavy stuff; it also included happiness and excitement.

The power of sharing became evident as each friend expressed themselves. Sophie noticed how her friends looked more relaxed as they spoke. They were learning that they could trust each other with their feelings. Sophie felt proud that her first step toward sharing had helped create this space for everyone to be honest about their emotions. This experience strengthened their friendship.

As the weeks went by, Sophie and her friends made it a habit to have these open discussions. They set aside time every Friday evening for what they called "Feelings Hour." They would gather in each other's houses, share snacks, and talk. Sometimes they played games, but the heart of their time together remained focused on sharing their feelings. They celebrated good news, like when Emma got a great score on her test or when Tom achieved a personal goal. They also supported one another during tough times, like when Sophie faced challenges with her family or when Emma felt down.

The school counselor noticed the change in Sophie and encouraged her to continue exploring her emotions. Sophie learned about healthy ways to cope with feelings. She discovered mindfulness exercises like deep breathing, which helped calm her when she felt overwhelmed. She also started practicing gratitude by writing down things she was grateful for each day. This shifted her focus from negative thoughts to positive experiences, which brightened her outlook on life.

Sophie became an advocate for sharing emotions among her peers. She even organized a small workshop at school where students could come together to talk about their feelings in a supportive environment. The workshop included icebreakers, games, and activities that encouraged open dialogue. It was a great success, and many students told Sophie how much they appreciated having a space to share.

By building this community, Sophie felt empowered. She learned that being vulnerable is not a weakness but a strength. Talking about feelings became easier, and it formed a bond between her and her friends. They realized they were not alone in their experiences, and this realization provided comfort. Sophie's journey taught her not only about her feelings but also about the importance of empathy.

Throughout this chapter of her life, Sophie discovered that everyone struggles with emotions in their own way. She learned to listen to her friends without judgment and to be there for them when they needed support. These relationships flourished as they practiced talking to one another openly. Suddenly, expressing feelings didn't seem daunting anymore; it was a natural and essential part of their friendship.

In sharing their experiences, they created a safe space to express anything, from silly to serious topics. The laughter that echoed during their conversations became a sound Sophie cherished. It was a reminder of how far she had come since that first meeting with the counselor. Looking back, Sophie understood that learning to talk about feelings was an ongoing journey. She embraced it, knowing that expressing her emotions not only helped herself but also strengthened her connections with others.

As Sophie continued to explore her emotions, she cultivated friendships that were deep and genuine. Everyone in the group felt a sense of belonging, and this made them more resilient when faced with life's challenges. They learned that talking about their feelings helped lift the weight off not just their shoulders but also each other's. Sophie had transformed her initial struggle into a powerful tool for connection and growth.

Chapter 5: The Magic of Mindfulness

Sophie sat in her counselor's office, feeling overwhelmed by the chaos in her mind. It was a typical day for her, filled with racing thoughts and a whirlwind of emotions. Her counselor, noticing her distress, decided to introduce her to a concept that could help. This idea was called **mindfulness**. Sophie was curious but uncertain about how this practice could really make a difference in her life. The counselor explained that mindfulness is all about staying in the moment. It helps people focus on the now, rather than getting lost in thoughts about the past or future.

Mindfulness can serve as a useful tool for many people. It allows individuals to step back from their thoughts and take a breath. Sophie learned that one of the most common ways to practice mindfulness is through simple breathing exercises. Her counselor suggested starting with a technique known as deep breathing. Sophie had never really thought about how she breathed before.

It seemed basic, but there was more to it than she realized.

To begin, Sophie found a comfortable spot to sit. She closed her eyes gently, allowing her body to relax. The counselor guided her to breathe in deeply through her nose. Sophie took a slow, deep breath, feeling her belly rise as she inhaled. She then learned to hold that breath for just a moment. Once she felt ready, she slowly exhaled through her mouth. As she released the breath, she imagined letting go of the tension that had been building up inside her. The counselor emphasized the importance of focusing only on these breaths, making it clear that this was her time to be present with herself.

After a few rounds of deep breathing, Sophie noticed a subtle change. The swirling thoughts in her mind began to settle down, like leaves calming in a gentle breeze. This feeling of relaxation felt strange but welcome. She asked her counselor how often she should practice these exercises. The counselor suggested starting with just a few minutes each day. Gradually, Sophie could increase the time as she got more comfortable. This seemed manageable, so she decided to give it a try.

In the following days, Sophie made a commitment to practice daily. She found a quiet corner in her home where she could sit without distraction. Sometimes, she lit a candle to set a peaceful atmosphere. Other times, she would play soft background music. These small rituals helped her to create a space where she could focus solely on her breathing. Sophie learned that being consistent was key. Yet, it was also important to be gentle with herself if she missed a day. Life can get busy, and that was completely okay.

As she continued her practice, Sophie began to notice additional benefits. Mindfulness not only helped her with her breathing but also encouraged her to observe her surroundings. Whenever she took a moment to step outside, she brought her attention to the beauty of nature. She watched the leaves flutter in the wind and listened to the chirping of birds. This simple practice of observation grounded her even more. It reminded her to find joy in little things that she often overlooked.

Sophie also discovered mindful eating. This was a new concept for her. She learned to pay attention to the taste, texture, and smell of her food. Instead of hurrying through meals while scrolling on her phone, Sophie took her time. She savored each bite, fully experiencing her food. This not only made her meals more enjoyable but also made her feel more satisfied. It helped her become aware of her body's hunger and fullness signals, allowing her to eat more intuitively.

Another beneficial practice Sophie started was mindfulness walking. On some days, she would take a walk in the park. During these walks, she focused on her steps and the sensation of her feet touching the ground. She noticed how the fresh air felt against her skin and how the sun warmed her face. Mindfulness walking became a way for her to connect with her body and the environment around her. Each walk was different, and she learned that being present during these moments was all that mattered.

Over time, Sophie found mindfulness becoming a natural part of her daily routine. She realized that it wasn't just about specific exercises; it was about a mindset. Mindfulness encouraged her to face her emotions without judgment. When challenging feelings would pop up, she learned not to push them away but to simply acknowledge them. This was a profound shift for her.

One day, Sophie felt a wave of anxiety wash over her unexpectedly. Instead of feeling overwhelmed like usual, she remembered her counselor's words. She took a moment to breathe, focusing on the breath flowing in and out. She allowed herself to be present with her feelings and didn't rush to fix them. This was a turning point in her understanding of mindfulness. She realized that it provided a safe space to sit with discomfort, rather than avoiding it.

The more Sophie practiced mindfulness, the deeper her understanding became. She learned that it wasn't always easy. Some days were harder than others, but she was willing to face that challenge. Mindfulness taught her patience and self-compassion. It encouraged her to show kindness to herself. Whenever she made a mistake or felt low, she would remind herself that it's okay to struggle. This awareness was empowering.

Sophie also sought out mindfulness resources to deepen her practice. She started reading books and watching videos about mindfulness techniques. She found guided meditations that resonated with her. Each resource offered new insights and approaches that enriched her experience. Experimenting with different practices allowed her to find what worked best for her.

She also began sharing her experience with friends. Sophie organized small gatherings where they could practice mindfulness together. They took turns leading breathing exercises and mindfulness walks. The support and camaraderie from these shared practices created a welcoming space for everyone. This connection enhanced her practice, allowing them all to learn from each other's experiences.

Sophie realized that mindfulness was not just about calming her mind. It was about developing a deeper connection to herself and the world around her. With continued exploration, she saw how mindfulness could influence various aspects of her life. It provided the tools to face challenges with clarity.

One evening while journaling, Sophie reflected on her journey with mindfulness.

She recognized how much growth had occurred since first learning from her counselor. Mindfulness had opened up pathways for self-discovery. It was a tool she could carry with her anywhere. She felt grateful for this practice and the shifts it had brought to her life. As Sophie looked ahead, she was excited to continue exploring the magic of mindfulness. The journey was just beginning, and she felt equipped to embrace whatever came next.

Chapter 6: Breathing Through the Storm

Sophie woke up that day with a knot in her stomach. A school presentation awaited her, and the thought of standing in front of her classmates made her anxious. She could feel her heart racing and her palms sweating. The anxiety wrapped around her like a heavy blanket. As she got ready for school, she tried to focus on the contents of her presentation, but her mind kept wandering to the thought of speaking in front of everyone. She remembered how difficult it had been to speak in public in the past and how fear had held her back.

At school, the anxiety grew stronger as she walked toward the classroom. Other students were chatting, but Sophie felt detached from them. She felt as if she were in a bubble, and the noise around her faded into the background. The closer she got to her presentation, the more her stomach twisted. Sophie needed a way to cope with these feelings. That's when she remembered the breathing techniques her teacher had shared in class a few months earlier. Learning about these techniques had been helpful, and now she needed to apply them.

Sophie took a deep breath, filling her lungs with air, and slowly exhaled. She focused on her breath, letting the worries slip away with each exhale. Inhale deeply through the nose for four counts, hold the breath for four more counts, and then exhale slowly through the mouth for six counts. This technique brought her a sense of calm that reminded her of the ocean waves—smooth and soothing. Even though she was still feeling anxious, she understood that controlling her breath could help her feel more centered and ready.

As she approached the classroom, Sophie practiced this technique a few more times. She found a quiet spot near her classroom door where she could focus. Inhale… one, two, three, four. Hold… one, two, three, four. Exhale… one, two, three, four, five, six. With each breath, the tightness in her chest began to loosen. Sophie discovered that breathing was not just something we do; it's a way to connect our mind and body.

It is a bridge that allows us to manage our emotions and regain balance.

When the teacher called her name, Sophie felt the adrenaline surge again. She stepped forward, but this time, she took a moment to pause at the front of the class. Instead of rushing in, she remembered her breathing exercises and let that be her guide. She took another deep breath before starting her presentation. This momentary pause not only helped settle her nerves but also gave her a moment to gather her thoughts.

As she began to speak, Sophie noticed the importance of making eye contact with her classmates. It helped her feel more connected to them. She saw familiar faces; some smiled back at her, while others appeared focused. This interaction made it easier for her to share her ideas. With each word she spoke, she felt more confidence building. When she stumbled on a few words, she breathed deeply and regained her composure. Instead of letting the anxiety take over, she reminded herself that it was normal to make mistakes.

Sophie had also learned that sometimes, sharing a personal story related to her topic could capture her classmates' attention. She told them about a time she faced a challenge similar to the topic of her presentation. This made her feel more relaxed and humanized the experience. Students could relate to her struggles, which helped to break the ice. The laughter that followed brought a sense of warmth in the room.

As she wrapped up her presentation, Sophie felt proud of herself. The storm of nerves she had initially felt transformed into a sense of accomplishment. She used her breathing techniques effectively, allowing herself to enjoy the process. The experience had taught her that she could control her anxiety, and it was possible to face public speaking with confidence.

Sophie left the classroom feeling lighter. She didn't just overcome her fear but also learned the power of managing her anxiety through simple techniques. When she reflected on the day, it was incredible to realize how much had changed by just focusing on her breath. Breathing through challenges can often feel like an overpowering task, but it can turn into a comforting ritual if we allow it.

After that day, Sophie made a commitment to incorporate breathing exercises into her daily routine. She understood the significance of staying calm and focused, especially as she moved forward in school and life. Whether it was during exams, sports events, or other presentations, she knew that she could rely on her breathing to help her find ease amidst the storm.

Her friends began to notice the change in her. Sophie started sharing her experience with them, explaining how breathing helped her manage anxiety. They were curious and wanted to know more, so Sophie decided to teach them the technique she had learned. They practiced together, and soon her group of friends formed a supportive community. When one felt anxious about a test, others would join in and breathe alongside them. This shared experience strengthened their friendship and built their confidence collectively.

Sophie learned that breathing wasn't just a personal tool but a bond that connected her with others. They all faced pressures in school, and knowing they could support one another through breathing made a difference. It turned into a way to encourage each other, share successes, and reflect on their challenges. Before long, the group found additional techniques they could explore together, like stretching and mindfulness activities, which further enriched their emotional resilience.

Through it all, Sophie realized how important it is to embrace vulnerability. It was empowering to share her experience and understand that everyone has their storms to weather. By remaining open, they created an environment where people could express their feelings and recognize that they weren't alone. This openness also fostered a culture where everyone felt comfortable asking for help or guidance during difficult times.

As the weeks progressed, Sophie became a role model for others. She inspired her classmates to engage in breathing exercises before class presentations or tests. When her teacher noticed this positive change in the classroom atmosphere, she decided to introduce mindfulness practices regularly. With each session, more students began to see the benefits of focusing on breath and being present in the moment. Sophie had started a wave of change, one breath at a time.

This journey was significant for Sophie. It was no longer just about overcoming her anxiety; it was about creating a community built on support, understanding, and the power of breathing together. Each day brought new challenges and experiences, but now she viewed them with a sense of calm determination. Whenever life threw a storm her way, Sophie knew she had the tools to breathe through it.

Chapter 7: The Power of Gratitude

Sophie decides to start a gratitude journal, a simple but powerful tool that encourages people to reflect on what they appreciate in their lives. Each day, she dedicates a few minutes to write down the things she is thankful for. This practice can be done in the morning to set a positive tone for the day or in the evening to reflect on the day's events. The act of writing helps Sophie focus her thoughts on the positives rather than any negative experiences she may have faced.

Throughout her journey with the gratitude journal, Sophie begins to notice changes in her mood. At first, it seems challenging to come up with items to list, especially on days when life feels particularly heavy.

However, she quickly learns that gratitude doesn't always have to be about big events. It can be as simple as enjoying a warm cup of coffee or hearing a favorite song on the radio. This realization opens her eyes to the many small joys in her everyday life. Each item she writes down adds up, creating a collection of memories and experiences that lighten her heart.

To make the most of her gratitude journal, Sophie develops a routine. She sets aside time each day in a quiet space where she can think without distractions. This could be a cozy corner of her room or a comfortable chair in her living room. She also picks a nice journal that she enjoys writing in, which makes the act feel special. Sophie emphasizes the importance of consistency. By setting a specific time, whether it's after breakfast or right before bed, she turns writing into a habit.

In her journal, Sophie categorizes her entries into different areas of her life. One day might focus on family, while another could highlight friends or work achievements. This division allows her to explore gratitude in various contexts, showing her that appreciation can come from many sources. For example, she might write about a meaningful conversation with her sister or the support of her colleagues during a tough project. These varied prompts inspire deeper thoughts and foster a broader sense of thankfulness.

Sophie also understands that gratitude isn't just a one-way street; it can encourage connection and bring people closer together. When she reflects on something that makes her feel thankful, she often reaches out to the person involved. For instance, if she writes about her friend who always makes her laugh, she takes the time to send a text or give them a call. This strengthens their bond and fosters a sense of community, making Sophie even more aware of her supportive relationships.

To deepen her practice, Sophie occasionally reviews her past entries. Looking back on what she has written reminds her of all the good times she has experienced. It also highlights her growth over time. During moments when she feels low, she revisiting happy memories can help lift her spirits. She finds joy in recalling experiences that sparked happiness, reminding her of the beautiful aspects of life she may overlook in challenging times. With each reflection, Sophie builds a resilience that helps her face life's ups and downs.

Sophie learns to appreciate not just the pleasant experiences but also the lessons learned from hardships. She realizes that even difficult situations can yield valuable insights. For example, she reflects on a challenging work project that pushed her to her limits. Although the stress was significant, she acknowledges how it taught her time management and teamwork skills. By recognizing the silver linings in tough times, Sophie broadens her understanding of gratitude, allowing it to become a more holistic practice.

The act of nurturing gratitude also encourages Sophie to practice mindfulness. Each night before she goes to bed, she takes a few moments to pay attention to her breath. This moment of stillness helps her ground her thoughts before transitioning into her gratitude writing. She learns to be present in the moment, appreciating the here and now.

Sophie finds that mindfulness enhances her gratitude practice, as she becomes more aware of her feelings, surroundings, and experiences.

Through her ongoing journey with the gratitude journal, Sophie begins to notice shifts in her overall well-being. The weight of stress seems lighter, and her outlook on life improves. She feels more optimistic and open to challenges that come her way. This positive change isn't just about how she feels day-to-day; it also influences how she interacts with others. As her mindset shifts toward gratitude, she feels more inclined to celebrate others' successes instead of comparing herself to them. This change in perspective fosters a deeper sense of fulfillment.

Sophie finds ways to incorporate gratitude into her daily conversations.

She starts by sharing her recent entries with friends and family. This invites them to participate in gratitude discussions, sparking deeper connections. Around the dinner table, she encourages everyone to mention one thing they are thankful for that day. This practice creates a warm environment filled with positivity and reinforces the idea that everyone has something to be grateful for, no matter how small.

Sophie occasionally explores gratitude beyond her personal journal. She participates in community service and begins to volunteer regularly. Through her service, she sees how appreciative gestures, even in small forms, can create significant impacts. For instance, she participates in organizing a food drive. The gratitude expressed by the recipients strengthens her resolve to be a part of something bigger than herself. This experience matures her understanding of gratitude, morphing it into a broader social practice.

Moreover, Sophie discovers the power of gratitude in difficult moments. When faced with challenges, she tries to find or create some good in uncomfortable situations. If she has a tough day at work, she consciously seeks out a helpful lesson from the experience instead of lingering on the negativity. This approach helps her cope and fosters a more resilient mindset. Sophie realizes that integrating gratitude into struggles allows her not just to accept challenges but to embrace them head-on.

In time, Sophie shares her experiences and newfound knowledge about gratitude with others. She starts a small group where participants discuss and share their gratitude practices. Together, they explore various creativity aspects, such as writing, art, or spoken word, to express thanks. This collective environment encourages open sharing and enhances each person's understanding of gratitude. By fostering a community engaged in positivity, Sophie helps create a ripple effect that showcases the power of gratitude beyond her own life.

Ultimately, Sophie's gratitude journey becomes a foundation for personal growth and well-being. The journal she started evolves into a treasured companion that documents her evolution. Through gratitude, she discovers that it is not merely about counting blessings but rather cultivating a mindset that embraces life with all its ups and downs. This transformation resonates in her life every day as she continues to seek and share appreciation in various forms, finding joy in the small and big things alike.

Chapter 8: Recognizing Stress

Sophie sits in her classroom, surrounded by her classmates, who seem equally curious. Today, they are learning about something that touches everyone's lives: stress. Stress is a response that the body has when it feels overwhelmed. It can come from many places, such as school, family, or even friendships. Understanding what stress is and how it can affect both the mind and body is essential. For Sophie, this lesson opens a door to new possibilities.

The teacher begins by introducing the concept of stress. "Stress is our body's way of reacting to a challenge," she explains. Sophie listens intently as the teacher continues, detailing how stress can make people feel anxious or tired. It affects the brain, leading to trouble focusing or sleeping. The teacher encourages the students to share moments when they felt stressed. Sophie raises her hand and shares how she feels before a big exam. This connection also helps her classmates relate their experiences, creating an environment where feelings are validated.

Next, the teacher explains that stress isn't just mental; it also impacts the body. Sophie learns that, when stressed, some may experience headaches or stomach aches. The body reacts by increasing heart rate and tension in the muscles. To help everyone understand, the teacher plays a short video that shows how stress triggers these responses. The visual aids are helpful, making the information more concrete. It's one thing to hear about stress, but seeing the mechanics makes it clearer.

To combat stress, the teacher shares some fun and effective ways to reduce it. Stretching is introduced as a simple exercise that everyone can do. The teacher stands up and demonstrates a few stretches, encouraging the students to follow along. Sophie stretches her arms high above her head and then leans to the side. She feels a sense of relief in her muscles, and it makes her smile. Stretching feels good, and Sophie thinks about how she could do this at home too.

Next, the class discusses drawing as a tool for stress relief. The teacher encourages them to express their feelings on paper. "Drawing is a way to let out what is inside," she says. Sophie loves art, and this suggestion excites her. The idea that she can put her thoughts and worries onto paper opens up a new outlet for her emotions. The teacher hands out coloring pages and colored pencils, and the classroom buzzes with creativity. Sophie picks bright colors to fill in her drawing, feeling the stress of the day melt away with each stroke.

Listening to music is another method Sophie learns about. The teacher explains how music can change moods and help one feel calmer. She encourages the students to create a "calm playlist" with their favorite soothing songs. Sophie thinks about the music she enjoys and decides to create her playlist at home. This idea excites her because she knows that music has the power to make her happy or relaxed.

As the lesson goes on, the teacher encourages the students to talk about the importance of recognizing stress signals. Understanding when stress happens is key to managing it. Sophie learns that by being aware of her feelings and body reactions, she can better address her stress. The teacher suggests keeping a journal to track these feelings, which is another way to clear the mind. Sophie finds this suggestion interesting. Writing down her thoughts seems like a good tool to help her understand what she's going through.

The teacher emphasizes that it's okay to feel stress. Everyone experiences it at different points in life, and what works for one person may not work for another. This notion reassures Sophie. She appreciates knowing that her feelings are normal and that she is not alone in her experiences. They discuss other ways to manage stress when it arises. Practicing deep breathing is introduced as a helpful technique.

"Taking a moment to breathe deeply can really help," the teacher says. She explains that when feeling stressed, one can close their eyes, breathe in through the nose for a count of four, hold the breath for four counts, and then let it out slowly through the mouth. Sophie tries this along with her classmates. She finds that it really does help her feel calmer. It's like hitting the reset button in her mind, allowing her to think more clearly.

As the class continues, Sophie reflects on how stress appears in her daily routine. She realizes that during tricky homework assignments, she often feels the pressure. By recognizing these moments, Sophie feels empowered. She believes that by applying the techniques discussed, she can manage her stress better. It's about being aware and using the tools available.

The lesson wraps up with the teacher encouraging everyone to share what they found most helpful. Sophie raises her hand and excitedly mentions how stretching felt refreshing. Other students agree, sharing their insights about drawing and music. The class buzzes with energy as everyone acknowledges that they have found their own ways to cope.

Before leaving, the teacher reminds them that practicing these techniques routinely can make them more effective. Sophie thinks this is wise advice. Just like homework, stress management also requires practice to improve skills.

At the end of the day, Sophie feels more equipped to handle her stress. The class's discussions and activities have opened her eyes to new methods. She considers what she will do at home: create her calm playlist, try stretching during study breaks, and start a journal. With these strategies, Sophie feels hopeful and determined to embrace this knowledge, knowing it will help her navigate school and life better.

As she walks home, Sophie processes everything she has learned. Stress is now a familiar concept, one that she understands deeply. Each tool she picked up that day feels valuable. It's not just about acknowledging stress; it's about managing it in a healthy way. Sophie is excited about her new knowledge, ready to take on any challenges that come her way, one stretched muscle at a time.

Chapter 9: Managing Friendships

Sophie has always valued her friendships. However, she finds herself facing several challenges that make her feel lonely. This loneliness can be difficult to understand. It's not just the absence of friends; it's also a sense of disconnect from those she cares about. Sophie starts to notice that some of her friendships are not as strong as she thought. They begin to feel more like obligations than meaningful connections. For instance, when she wants to spend time with her closest friend, she often feels brushed off or ignored. This leads her to question the quality of her relationships and her worth as a friend.

As Sophie navigates this emotional landscape, she begins to learn about conflict. Conflicts often arise in friendships, and they can stem from misunderstandings, disagreements, or unmet expectations. Sophie realizes that when she feels neglected, it's important to communicate her feelings rather than harbor resentment. An example of this could be a situation where she feels left out of group activities. Instead of keeping quiet, Sophie decides to approach her friends and express her feelings. She learns that having an open dialogue about her emotions helps clear misunderstandings. This step, though challenging, becomes a crucial point in her journey of managing friendships.

Another important lesson Sophie discovers is the significance of setting boundaries. Without boundaries, friendships can become chaotic and lead to feelings of being overwhelmed. Sophie starts by evaluating her own needs in her friendships. She thinks about what she can handle and what drains her energy. For instance, if a friend consistently calls her late at night for advice, Sophie realizes that she needs to set a limit on when she is available to talk. She decides to communicate this to her friend, explaining that while she values their conversations, she needs to set aside specific times when she can focus fully. This clear communication not only helps Sophie feel more in control but also allows her friend to understand her limits better.

Sophie also learns about the importance of reciprocity in friendships. Friendships thrive on mutual support. If one person is always giving while the other is taking, it can lead to imbalance and resentment. Sophie starts to assess her friendships to see if they align with this principle. In one instance, she notices that she is frequently the one reaching out to make plans, while her friends rarely initiate. This realization prompts her to address the issue. She reaches out to her friends and shares her observations. By encouraging them to take the lead once in a while, she fosters a sense of equal partnership in her relationships. This shift solidifies her friendships and enhances her feelings of belonging.

As Sophie navigates her friendships, she becomes acutely aware of the types of connections she wants to maintain. She reflects on her values and how they align with her friends. For example, she considers whether her friends share similar interests or support her goals. By surrounding herself with friends who lift her up and inspire her, Sophie feels a renewed sense of positivity. When she spends time with people who appreciate her for who she is, her feelings of loneliness diminish significantly. Sophie makes a conscious effort to seek out friendships that feel genuine and fulfilling.

In addition, Sophie realizes the importance of making time for her friends. Life can get busy, but prioritizing friendships is essential for emotional well-being. To do this, she creates a schedule that includes regular Friend Dates. These dates could be as simple as grabbing coffee, taking a walk, or having a movie night. By carving out time for her friends, Sophie strengthens those connections. She also encourages her friends to be involved in planning these gatherings. This not only takes the pressure off her but also fosters a sense of shared responsibility.

Conflict resolution becomes an essential skill for Sophie as she continues to manage her friendships. As she encounters disagreements, she learns to handle them with grace and understanding. Instead of allowing conflicts to fester, she practices active listening. When a disagreement arises, she allows her friend to express their perspective fully before sharing her own. This collaborative approach often leads to resolutions that satisfy both parties. For example, if there is a misunderstanding regarding who is organizing a group event, Sophie suggests discussing it openly, rather than assigning blame. By emphasizing collaborative problem-solving, they strengthen their friendship and build trust.

Sophie also learns the value of forgiveness in friendships. No one is perfect, and misunderstandings will happen. When a friend hurts her feelings unintentionally, Sophie realizes that holding onto anger only weighs her down. Instead, she reflects on the situation and decides to talk to her friend about it. By addressing the hurt directly, she gives them a chance to apologize and make amends. Forgiveness does not mean forgetting; it means allowing space for healing in the relationship. This sense of understanding allows her to move forward without holding onto unnecessary baggage.

In Sophie's journey, she also discovers that friendships can evolve. People change over time, and sometimes friendships fade or grow apart. Instead of clinging to friendships that no longer serve her, she learns to accept this natural progression. This acceptance allows Sophie to free herself from the guilt of losing friends. She realizes that it is possible to cherish past connections while letting go of those that no longer fit into her life. By embracing this fluidity, she creates room for new friendships that align better with her current self.

Throughout her journey of managing friendships, Sophie also recognizes the importance of self-care. Valuing herself and taking care of her own emotional needs helps her be a better friend. She begins to engage in activities that bring her joy, such as reading, exercising, or pursuing creative hobbies. This self-focus nurtures her spirit, making her more available and present in her friendships. When she takes time for herself, she finds that she has more to offer her friends, leading to healthier, more balanced relationships.

Lastly, as Sophie continues to grow and learn, she becomes an advocate for her friends as well. She encourages them to communicate their feelings and set boundaries. By sharing her experiences and the lessons she's learned, she inspires those around her to embrace healthy friendship practices. This ripple effect helps to create a supportive network where friends uplift one another. Sophie's journey of managing friendships becomes not only a personal transformation but also a shared experience with those she cares about. Her connections grow stronger, more authentic, and deeply fulfilling.

Chapter 10: The Importance of Rest

Sophie had been feeling drained lately. She found herself yawning at the most unexpected moments and struggling to keep her eyes open during her favorite TV show. One day, she looked at her reflection in the mirror and noticed dark circles under her eyes. It was clear to her that she wasn't getting enough sleep. This realization pushed her to think about how important rest truly was.

Learning about the importance of rest was a revelation for Sophie. She discovered that sleep was not just about feeling tired or refreshed the next day. It played a crucial role in her mental and emotional health. Studies suggested that getting a good night's sleep could improve focus, memory, and mood. It was fascinating to see how the mind and body worked together, and sleep was a significant part of that equation.

To understand rest better, Sophie dove into the fundamentals of sleep. She found out that sleep consists of various cycles, including light sleep, deep sleep, and REM sleep. Each stage has its importance. For instance, deep sleep helps the body recover and build energy, while REM sleep allows for processing emotions and memories. Sophie realized how complex yet vital these stages were for her overall well-being.

Sophie wanted to improve her sleep habits. She decided to talk to her parents about her struggle. They were supportive and shared their own experiences. Her mom mentioned how, when she was younger, she would stay up late watching movies and often felt tired the next day. Sophie listened keenly as her mom described how she learned to set a consistent bedtime and wake-up time. This routine made a huge difference in her life.

With her parents' help, Sophie started to create a bedtime routine. They sat down together to write out what needed to change. First, they agreed on a specific time for her to go to bed each night. It was essential to stick to that time even on weekends. Sophie understood that this consistency helped regulate her internal clock. Her dad suggested using an alarm to remind her when it was time to start winding down for the evening.

Next, Sophie worked on creating a calm environment in her bedroom. She learned that a dark, quiet room is ideal for sleep. Her parents helped her set up heavy curtains to block out light and encouraged her to turn off electronic devices at least an hour before bed. Sophie found comfort in reading a book instead. She was excited to discover new stories without the distraction of screens.

Another part of her new routine involved relaxing activities before bed. Sophie's dad suggested gentle stretching or yoga. He explained that physical relaxation can signal the body it's time to rest. They spent a few minutes each night stretching together, which helped ease the tension in Sophie's muscles. She found it enjoyable to connect with her dad like that.

Sophie also learned about the importance of skipping big meals or sugary snacks close to bedtime. Her mom explained that heavy foods could lead to discomfort during the night. Instead, they started preparing light snacks like fruits or yogurt in the evening. Sophie liked this change; it made her feel healthier and more energized.

To further enhance her nighttime routine, Sophie decided to keep a journal. Every night, she spent a few minutes writing down her thoughts and feelings. This helped her process the day and let go of anything weighing heavily on her mind. Writing became a soothing ritual, making it easier for her to relax before bedtime.

Over time, Sophie noticed changes in how she felt. She became more alert at school and could concentrate better in class. Her grades began to improve, and she felt happier overall. This experience taught her that taking care of her body and mind was not only important but necessary. The effects of proper rest extended far beyond just feeling sleepy.

With newfound energy, Sophie decided to share her journey with friends. She spoke to them about how setting a bedtime routine helped her and emphasized the importance of rest. Some of her friends were intrigued and wanted to try it too. Sophie encouraged them to start small, like choosing a bedtime and limiting screen time.

Sophie's journey with rest inspired her to explore other self-care practices. She became curious about mindfulness and meditation. A friend shared guided meditations that could help calm the mind before bed. Sophie was excited about this new area to explore. She started incorporating short meditation sessions into her routine, which further enriched her relaxation time.

As Sophie developed these habits, she realized that asking for help is okay when you're struggling. Her parents had been a huge support for her, and she felt grateful for their guidance. This opened her eyes to the idea that self-care was not just a personal journey; it also involved connections with others.

Learning about the importance of rest changed Sophie's life significantly. She gained a sense of control over her well-being and developed habits that would serve her well into the future. This chapter of her life was a powerful reminder that rest is not just a luxury for some, but a necessity for everyone.

Through her journey, Sophie discovered tools she could use to manage stress and prioritize her needs. Whether it's a carefully crafted bedtime routine, journaling her thoughts, or simply stretching before bed, she felt more equipped to tackle daily challenges. Each step was a building block leading to a healthier, well-rested version of herself.

As time went on and Sophie continued to nurture her sleep habits, she also became more aware of her overall health. She began to think about how the food she consumed and the activities she engaged in during the day affected her nights. Slowly, she started making healthier choices in her diet and became more active. This holistic approach left her feeling revitalized and ready to sleep peacefully each night.

Sophie's commitment to improving her sleep showed her that change takes time, but it's worth the effort. Her experience encouraged her friends, too. They began discussing how they felt and sharing what worked for them. This became a bonding experience, as they all learned the value of rest together.

In the end, Sophie gained more than just better sleep habits; she found a supportive community and learned about the importance of cherishing her time for rest. It was a meaningful journey filled with small victories and lasting change. Each night she snuggled into her bed, she was grateful for the path she had taken toward better rest.

Chapter 11: Finding Your Safe Space

Sophie discovers a unique comfort in the outdoors, particularly when surrounded by nature. The fresh air, gentle sounds, and beautiful vistas create a peaceful environment that helps her feel calm and happy. This realization motivates her to seek out outdoor spaces more often. Among these, she finds a special park that resonates deeply with her. This park quickly becomes her safe space.

The park is filled with tall trees and vibrant flowers, offering a picturesque scene. Each visit allows Sophie to reconnect with herself, away from the distractions of daily life. She notices how the sunlight filters through the leaves, casting playful shadows on the ground. The soft rustling of leaves and the occasional chirping of birds bring her a sense of tranquility. It is in this park that she can let go of her worries and focus on what truly matters.

To make the most of her time in the park, Sophie establishes a routine. Each weekend, she sets aside a few hours to visit. She packs a light backpack with her favorlte blanket, a good book, and some snacks. By doing this, she creates a mini escape where she can immerse herself in the serenity of nature. On her first visit, she finds a cozy spot under a large oak tree. Spreading out the blanket, she sits down and takes a deep breath, feeling the calm wash over her.

The act of simply being outside helps Sophie to reflect on her thoughts. She finds that writing in a journal is a great way to process her feelings. On her visits, she brings her journal along and takes time to jot down her thoughts. Writing helps her understand her emotions and clear her mind. As she looks around the park, she writes about the sights and sounds, capturing her experience in words.

Sometimes, Sophie chooses to engage in mindful walking. This involves walking slowly and paying close attention to the environment around her. With each step, she notices the texture of the ground beneath her feet and the scent of the flowers blooming nearby. This practice gives her a heightened awareness of the world. By focusing on the present moment, she finds it easier to leave her worries behind.

Sophie also enjoys observing the wildlife in the park. As she sits quietly, birds flit from branch to branch, and squirrels scurry along the ground. She becomes fascinated by their behaviors and the way they interact. This observation not only entertains her but also reminds her of the beauty of life happening all around her.

Her connection to nature deepens as she learns about the different plants and animals she encounters. She takes the time to research the species she sees in the park. By understanding their habits and habitats, she feels more engaged with her surroundings. This knowledge enhances her visits and helps her to appreciate the park even more.

Social connections also play a role in making the park her safe space. Sophie finds that inviting friends to join her enhances her experience. They share laughter and stories under the open sky, creating happy memories together. These social interactions provide a balance to her solitary moments, making her time in the park even more valuable.

Additionally, Sophie begins to practice yoga in her safe space. The calm atmosphere aids her concentration during her practice. She finds the movements flow better when she is in nature, and she is more aware of her breath. The sounds of the park become a soothing background as she flows through poses. Each session leaves her feeling rejuvenated, both physically and mentally.

Sophie also experiments with different activities to enrich her time in the park. Sometimes, she brings along art supplies. With a sketchbook and pencils, she sits quietly and begins to draw the scenery before her. The act of drawing helps her to see the world through a different lens. It teaches her patience and allows her to appreciate the details she may otherwise overlook.

Cooking outdoors becomes another delightful venture. Sophie learns to prepare simple meals using a portable stove. She enjoys the entire process, from gathering fresh ingredients at home to cooking in her park setting. The smells of the food mix with the fresh air, creating a sensory experience that brings her joy. Sharing these meals with friends adds another layer to her park visits.

As seasons change, so does her experience in the park. Each season offers something new, altering the landscape around her. In spring, blossoms burst forth in vibrant colors, while autumn brings a cascade of golden leaves. Sophie embraces these changes, reflecting on how they mirror her own life transitions. This understanding fosters a sense of growth within her.

Sometimes, during her visits, Sophie encounters challenges. On a particularly windy day, it becomes difficult to focus on her writing. Instead of getting frustrated, she decides to embrace the chaos. She observes how the wind bends the grasses and plays with the branches. By accepting the moment for what it is, she finds creativity in the unpredictability of nature.

Through all these experiences, the park transforms into more than just a physical space. It becomes an extension of her personal journey. Sophie learns to navigate her thoughts and feelings through nature, allowing her to face life's challenges with a clearer mind. Each visit reinforces her understanding of the importance of having a safe space, a place where she can be herself without judgment.

As time passes, the park remains a constant in her life. Sophie realizes that no matter where she goes, she can carry the essence of her safe space with her.

The lessons she learns in the park—mindfulness, creativity, acceptance—become tools she uses to face the outside world. Her connection to nature helps ground her in moments of uncertainty.

Sophie understands that finding your safe space can mean different things to different people. For some, it might be a cozy corner in their home, while for others, it could be a community garden. The key is to seek an environment that promotes peace and fosters reflection. By taking the time to identify and invest in these spaces, anyone can benefit from the calm they offer.

Ultimately, the personal journey of finding a safe space is one that continues to evolve. Sophie looks forward to her future visits to the park, knowing that each time will be a chance for renewal and growth.

The park represents a commitment to her well-being and a reminder of the joy that nature brings her on her journey.

Chapter 12: The Power of Positive Thinking

Sophie discovers that the way she talks to herself can have a big impact on her feelings and actions. She starts to notice that whenever she thinks or speaks negatively, it brings her down. For example, if she wakes up and immediately thinks, "I can't face this day," she feels tired and unmotivated. It becomes clear to her that her mindset can change her whole day. This revelation leads her to experiment with different phrases and thoughts.

To make this change, Sophie decides to practice positive thinking actively. She makes a list of negative thoughts that she often has. Phrases like "I'm not good enough" or "I will fail" are common on her list. She realizes that these thoughts are not just moments of self-doubt; they are toxic to her mindset. Sophie understands that she needs to replace these thoughts with something more uplifting. She starts writing down positive affirmations next to each negative phrase. For instance, next to "I can't do this," she writes "I'll give it my best shot."

By repeating her new positive phrases, Sophie feels a shift in her mindset. She carries her list around with her and reads it when she feels low. This simple act helps her to encourage herself throughout her day. For example, before a big presentation at work, instead of thinking, "What if I mess up?" She reminds herself, "I have prepared for this and I can handle it." This change in perspective offers her confidence.

Sophie also learns the importance of being patient with herself. Changing thought patterns does not happen overnight. Some days are harder than others. There are moments when she slips back into negativity, but she doesn't let it discourage her. Instead, she views these moments as opportunities to practice. When she catches herself thinking negatively, she pauses. Sophie takes a deep breath and consciously chooses to switch to a positive thought.

Another helpful tip Sophie discovers is the power of visualization. She begins to visualize success in her daily tasks. For instance, when preparing for a family gathering, she imagines the laughter, joy, and connection she will share with her loved ones. This practice makes her feel excited and less anxious about social situations. Visualization acts like a mental rehearsal, and the more she does it, the more comfortable she becomes.

Sophie also seeks out supportive people in her life. She talks to friends about her journey towards positive thinking. Some of them share their own experiences with negativity and how they overcame it. By sharing, they reinforce each other's positive efforts. Together, they create a small support group that meets regularly. They exchange motivational quotes, tips, and encouragement. Sophie realizes that having people who understand her goals makes a world of difference.

As Sophie continues on this path, she starts to notice real change. Tasks that once seemed overwhelming feel manageable. For example, tackling a difficult project at work doesn't fill her with dread anymore. Instead of thinking, "This will be impossible," she reminds herself,

"I can break this down into smaller tasks." This thought not only reduces her anxiety but allows her to approach the work systematically.

To further reinforce her positive thinking, Sophie incorporates gratitude into her daily routine. Every evening, she takes a moment to reflect on her day and jot down three things she is grateful for. These can be simple joys like the sun shining, a good cup of coffee, or a compliment from a colleague. This practice helps her focus on the positive aspects of her life, shifting her attention from what is lacking to what is abundant.

Sophie begins to see the cumulative effects of her changes. Over weeks and months, her confidence grows. Her positive outlook starts to influence her relationships and work life. Colleagues notice that her attitude has improved.

They appreciate her optimism, and some even ask her about her secret. She shares her experiences, encouraging them to try similar practices.

One day, she feels particularly brave and decides to take on a challenge she had previously avoided: public speaking. Sophie signs up for a local workshop. Before stepping on stage, she reminds herself of all the positive thoughts she practiced. Instead of picturing a room full of judging eyes, she imagines sharing her ideas with friends who are eager to listen. This mindset shift allows her to deliver her speech with confidence and passion.

Through her journey, Sophie learns that positive thinking is a skill, not merely a habit. It requires practice and commitment. Sophie sets aside time each week to read books and resources about self-improvement. She finds inspiration in stories of others who have transformed their mindsets. These readings motivate her to keep pushing forward.

She also starts to explore mindfulness and meditation as additional tools for maintaining positivity. Learning to sit quietly and focus on her breath helps her to clear her mind and reset. When negative thoughts creep in, she acknowledges them without judgment and lets them go. This process gives her a sense of peace and reminds her that thoughts are not facts.

Sophie's transformation becomes more evident. She engages more comfortably with others, tackles daily tasks with a sense of joy, and embraces challenges as opportunities to grow. As her positive thoughts start to shape her reality, she feels lighter and more optimistic. The change empowers her, and she realizes she can inspire others too.

The impact of positive thinking ripples through her life. It influences her decisions, relationships, and perceptions of herself. Sophie understands that this journey of positive thinking is ongoing. There will always be ups and downs, but she approaches each new day with a mindset that emphasizes growth, support, and gratitude. She learns that even when challenges arise, she is equipped with the tools and mindset to face them head-on.

Chapter 13: The Role of Food and Movement

Sophie has been paying attention to her body lately. She notices that when she chooses healthier foods, she feels more energized throughout the day. For example, instead of having sugary cereals for breakfast, she tries oatmeal topped with fresh fruit and nuts. This simple change makes a big difference in how she feels. Oatmeal gives her lasting energy, helping her stay focused in class. She learns that food is not just about taste; it affects her mood and energy levels as well.

Her gym teacher speaks about how important it is to connect food and movement. When Sophie asks for more details, her teacher explains that our bodies need fuel to function properly. This fuel comes from the food we eat. Just like a car needs gasoline to run, our bodies need nutritious food to perform well. Eating a balanced diet, which includes fruits, vegetables, whole grains, and proteins, can help Sophie feel better physically and mentally.

Sophie also discovers the importance of hydration. Drinking enough water is vital for her body to work optimally. She learns that when she is dehydrated, it can lead to fatigue and difficulty concentrating. Her gym teacher suggests keeping a water bottle nearby and taking regular sips throughout the day. This small change helps Sophie stay refreshed and alert during her activities.

As Sophie becomes more aware of her food choices, she decides to try cooking some healthy recipes at home. With her parents' help, she prepares a colorful salad filled with various vegetables. She includes tomatoes, cucumbers, and leafy greens, topped with a light vinaigrette. Not only does the salad taste great, but it also gives her a sense of accomplishment. Cooking allows her to take charge of what she eats, helping her make healthier choices.

In addition to food, Sophie learns that exercise plays a crucial role in her overall health. When she moves her body regularly, she feels happier and less stressed. For instance, after a brisk walk or a fun dance class, she notices a significant lift in her mood. Her heart beats faster, and she feels a rush of endorphins, often referred to as the "feel-good" hormones. This is a positive feedback loop—exercise leads to feeling good, which may lead to making better food choices.

Sophie's gym teacher emphasizes that any movement is beneficial. It doesn't have to be an intense workout at the gym. Simple activities like walking, biking, or playing a sport can make a big difference. Sophie reflects on how much she enjoys riding her bike with friends in the park. It's a fun way to exercise and bond with others at the same time.

She starts to set small fitness goals for herself. For instance, she aims to take a walk after dinner every evening. This routine not only helps with her physical health but also becomes a calming time for her to unwind after a long day. Walking outdoors allows her to appreciate nature and clear her mind, which enhances her mental well-being.

Sophie also finds that mixing different types of exercise keeps things interesting. She decides to sign up for a dance class at her school. Dancing is enjoyable and a great way for her to express herself while staying active. By varying her activities, she stays motivated and prevents boredom from creeping in.

Throughout this journey, Sophie connects with her friends and family. They share healthy recipes and motivate one another to stay active. For example, her family decides to have a "healthy cooking night" every week. They choose a new recipe to try together. Sharing this experience builds strong bonds and encourages everyone to maintain a healthy lifestyle.

In her health education classes, Sophie learns about the benefits of mental health in relation to physical health. Practicing mindfulness and relaxation techniques can help manage stress levels. For instance, deep breathing exercises or yoga can be great ways to calm the mind. Sophie integrates short mindfulness breaks into her daily routine. She finds that taking just a few moments to breathe deeply helps her refocus and feel more balanced.

Sophie also starts to understand nutrition labels on food packages. She becomes diligent about checking the ingredients and nutritional information when shopping with her parents. Knowing how to read labels empowers her to make healthier choices. She learns to look for items with whole ingredients and fewer processed components. This knowledge helps her navigate the grocery store with confidence.

In class, they discuss the importance of limiting sugary snacks and drinks. Sophie realizes that while treats are okay in moderation, they can lead to energy crashes if consumed too frequently. She decides to save sugary treats for special occasions. Instead, she seeks healthier alternatives, such as fruit or yogurt, to satisfy her sweet tooth.

With all this newfound knowledge, Sophie feels more in control of her health. She embraces the idea that food and movement work together to enhance her daily life. By fueling her body with nutritious foods and engaging in regular exercise, she notices overall improvements in her energy levels, mood, and focus.

Sophie becomes an advocate for healthy living among her friends. She shares tips on easy meal prep and fun activities to stay active. They form a small group dedicated to trying new recipes and exploring different forms of exercise, like hiking or yoga classes. This creates a supportive environment where everyone encourages each other to make healthier choices.

As time goes on, Sophie continues to learn and grow. She looks for ways to challenge herself, whether it's trying a new sport or experimenting with a new healthy recipe. With every step, she understands that this journey toward better health is ongoing. It involves making mindful decisions, staying active, and fostering connections with others through shared experiences.

Sophie has discovered the profound connection between food, movement, and mental well-being. She embraces her journey, acknowledging that both aspects are essential to a balanced life. This chapter in her life is just the beginning of a healthier, happier version of herself. Sophie looks forward to the future, ready to explore even more exciting possibilities in her quest for wellness.

Chapter 14: Dealing with Disappointment

Sophie was excited about the school soccer team. She had practiced hard, spent many afternoons kicking the ball in her backyard, and even watched videos to learn new skills. When the day came to try out for the team, her heart raced with hope. She imagined scoring goals and celebrating with her teammates.
However, when the results were posted, her name was not on the list.
Disappointment washed over her like a heavy blanket.

At first, Sophie couldn't believe it. She looked at the list again, thinking she might have missed it. But there it was, clear as day. She hadn't made the team. In that moment, her dreams felt shattered. Thoughts raced through her mind. She wondered if all her hard work had been for nothing. Why didn't she make it? Was she not good enough? Facing this disappointment was painful. It was like losing a part of her hopes.

As tears welled in her eyes, Sophie felt a mix of sadness and anger. It was okay to feel this way, she reminded herself. Everyone experiences disappointment at some point. It's a part of life. The key is how we deal with it. Sophie thought back to her friends and family. They often shared stories of their own disappointments. Her mom once told her about the time she didn't get into her dream college. Despite her hard work, she found herself at another school, but she learned so much and eventually found happiness in ways she didn't expect. That memory gave Sophie a little comfort.

After some time, she understood that disappointment is a natural emotion. Acknowledging her feelings was the first step. Sophie took a moment to sit down, breathe, and think. It felt good to let the sadness out rather than bottle it in. She decided to talk to her best friend, Anna. Friends can be a great support during tough times. Anna listened carefully as Sophie shared her feelings. Anna had experienced disappointment too, especially when she didn't get a role in the school play. They chatted, shared laughs, and comforted each other. This connection made Sophie feel less alone in her sadness.

Next, Sophie thought about what she could learn from this situation. She made a list of skills she wanted to improve. For instance, she wanted to work on her footwork and learn different strategies for playing soccer. Making a plan gave her a sense of control. It turned her disappointment into motivation. Sophie also reflected on her strengths. She loved soccer and enjoyed playing the game, whether in practice or with friends. This passion could guide her moving forward.

Setting specific goals was her next step. Maybe instead of focusing on making the team next year, she could join a local soccer club. This way, she could practice regularly, meet other players, and improve her skills. Joining a club would provide a new challenge and allow her to meet people who also loved soccer. Sophie felt excited about this idea. It was a chance to grow and learn without the pressure of a school team.

Sophie decided to reach out to a local soccer coach she had heard about. She looked up the details online and found the coach's contact information. Taking that step felt empowering. She wrote a friendly email, asking about practices and how she could join. This action helped move her forward and eased some of the heavy feelings of disappointment.

In the following weeks, Sophie focused on developing her skills. She practiced her footwork daily, using drills she had found online. For example, she created a mini obstacle course in her yard to help improve her agility. Each successful practice made her feel more confident. She began to see progress, and her excitement for the game returned.

Sophie also watched more soccer games on television. Analyzing how professional players moved and made decisions was helpful. She took notes on their strategies and even tried to imitate their techniques during her practice sessions. Watching these games fueled her passion and helped her understand the game more deeply. This approach turned her disappointment into something productive.

As summer approached, Sophie joined the local soccer club. She was nervous at first, as she didn't know anyone. But her excitement overcame her fear. At the first practice, she introduced herself and met other kids who loved soccer too. Everyone was friendly, and they welcomed her with open arms. The environment felt uplifting, which eased her worries. Not only was she playing soccer again, but she was also making new friends.

At the club, Sophie learned from various coaches, each offering unique insights and tips. They provided constructive feedback that helped her identify her weak points. This new focus made her more determined. She felt positive about her journey, reminding herself that everyone has setbacks and that what matters is finding a way to keep going.

Each practice became an opportunity to grow. Sophie set small goals for herself— like mastering a particular skill or improving her speed. These accomplishments built her confidence. With each milestone reached, Sophie learned to celebrate her progress. It reminded her that every small step was a victory in its own right.

Before she knew it, the fall season was approaching, and the school soccer team would hold tryouts again. This time, Sophie felt different. She wasn't just hoping to be picked; she had worked hard to develop her skills. The thought of trying out was no longer daunting. Instead, it felt exciting. If she didn't make the team again, she knew she'd still have the club and the skills she gained.

When tryout day arrived, Sophie walked onto the field feeling prepared. She played with confidence, showcasing the skills she had honed over the summer. Afterward, she felt proud of her performance, no matter the outcome. Eventually, when the results were posted, she discovered that her name was on the list. This moment filled her with immense joy, but also brought into focus the lessons she learned about handling disappointment.

Sophie realized that disappointment can be a stepping stone. It can teach valuable lessons and open new doors. Her journey showed her that while it's normal to feel sad, it's also vital to keep pushing forward. Disappointment can lead to growth and new opportunities if you approach it with the right mindset. Sophie learned to embrace her journey, grateful for every experience, good or bad, that shaped her into a stronger, more resilient person.

Chapter 15: Understanding Anxiety

Sophie had always been an active girl, full of curiosity and energy. But one day, while in the midst of a routine activity, she suddenly felt overwhelmed. Her heart started racing, her palms became sweaty, and she felt a tightness in her chest. This was a panic attack, and it left her shocked and confused. She couldn't understand why this was happening to her. It was a frightening experience, and she found herself thinking that something was seriously wrong.

Feeling scared and lost, Sophie decided to reach out for help. She talked to her counselor, a caring and knowledgeable person who made Sophie feel safe as she shared her experience. During their session, Sophie's counselor explained what anxiety truly is. Anxiety is more than just feeling stressed or worried; it's a natural response to a perceived threat. Everyone experiences anxiety at different levels, but for some, it can become overwhelming and impact daily life. It's essential to understand that it's okay to feel anxious; it's a common human experience.

The counselor went on to describe the different types of anxiety disorders. For instance, Generalized Anxiety Disorder (GAD) causes people to worry excessively about various aspects of life, often without a clear reason. Social Anxiety Disorder, on the other hand, makes individuals feel intense fear in social situations, worrying constantly about being judged by others. Panic Disorder can lead to repeated panic attacks, like the one Sophie experienced, creating a cycle of fear that can be very difficult to break.

Sophie listened closely, intrigued by the information. She learned that recognizing the signs of anxiety is the first step toward managing it. Some common signs include restlessness, irritability, muscle tension, difficulty concentrating, and sleep issues. By identifying these symptoms, individuals can become more aware of their anxious feelings and take proactive steps to address them.

To help Sophie cope, her counselor introduced her to various calming techniques. One of the first methods was deep breathing. This technique involves taking slow, deep breaths to help calm the body. Sophie practiced inhaling through her nose for four counts, holding her breath for four counts, and then exhaling through her mouth for six counts. This simple exercise allows the body to relax and reduce feelings of anxiety. "Whenever you feel anxious, just find a place to sit quietly and focus on your breathing," her counselor advised.

Another effective technique was progressive muscle relaxation. The counselor explained that this method involves tensing and then relaxing different muscle groups in the body, which can help release physical tension caused by anxiety. For example, Sophie was told to start by clenching her fists tightly for a few seconds and then letting them go. Moving through different parts of her body, she learned to pay attention to the sensations of tension and release. Practicing this regularly could help Sophie to feel more in control of her body and emotions.

Sophie also learned about mindfulness, which encourages being present in the moment without judgment. Her counselor suggested starting with short sessions, focusing on what she could see, hear, and feel around her. "Try to notice the little details," her counselor encouraged. "Look at the colors, notice the sounds, and pay attention to your feelings." This practice can reduce anxious thoughts by bringing attention back to the present moment.

As weeks passed, Sophie continued to meet with her counselor. Each session built on the last, providing her with more tools to handle her anxiety. Journaling was another suggestion. Writing about her feelings allowed Sophie to express herself and understand her thoughts better. She could write about her worries and then consider each one, often discovering that many were not as threatening as they initially seemed.

The counselor also emphasized the importance of a supportive social network. They discussed the significance of talking to trusted friends and family members about feelings of anxiety. Sophie learned that sharing her experiences could ease her burden and provide her with comfort. Friends could often offer different perspectives, and just having someone to listen can make a huge difference.

While Sophie learned these techniques, she also understood the power of routine. Having a regular schedule could provide structure and make life feel more predictable. Maintaining consistent sleep patterns, eating nutritious meals, and engaging in regular physical activity were all recommended as part of a healthy lifestyle. Simple exercises like walking, running, or yoga can decrease anxiety levels by releasing endorphins, which are chemicals in the brain that act as natural mood lifters.

The counselor highlighted that creating a calming environment at home can also significantly impact anxiety levels. Sophie started to declutter her space and make it more inviting. She added soft lighting and calming colors to her room, ensuring that she had a few cozy spots to retreat to when she needed to unwind. Having soothing items like a favorite blanket or candles could create a sense of peace in her environment.

Sophie was encouraged to celebrate her successes, no matter how small. Each time she managed a situation that made her nervous, she acknowledged it as a victory. Whether it was speaking in front of the class or trying something new, recognizing these moments helped build her confidence and resilience against anxiety.

As time went on, the panic attacks became less frequent. Sophie continued to practice her breathing techniques and skills learned from her counselor. She embraced her new tools with enthusiasm, integrating them into her daily life. Sophie realized that while anxiety might be a part of her experience, it no longer defined her. She learned that she could face challenges, armed with knowledge and techniques to support herself.

Through this journey, Sophie discovered that discussing anxiety openly helped to reduce the stigma surrounding it. She began sharing her experiences with her friends, encouraging them to talk about their feelings as well. This created a supportive atmosphere where they could all share strategies and provide comfort to one another.

Over time, Sophie's understanding of anxiety matured into a powerful lesson about resilience. Rather than running away from her anxious feelings, she learned to face them head-on. Instead of feeling ashamed, she found empowerment in acknowledging her struggles. Sophie's journey towards understanding anxiety turned into one of strength, and she continued to grow, support others, and share the tools that had helped her.

Chapter 16: The Strength of Vulnerability

Sophie sat in the living room, her heart pounding as she looked around at her family. They were engaged in a light-hearted conversation, laughing and sharing stories. Despite the cheerful atmosphere, Sophie felt a heavy weight pressing on her chest. She had been grappling with feelings of insecurity and worry for some time, and it was becoming increasingly difficult to keep it to herself. The more she tried to push her feelings down, the more they seemed to bubble up, leaving her feeling anxious and misunderstood.

Taking a deep breath, she realized it was time to be honest. Vulnerability felt scary, but she hoped it would bring her closer to her family. She spoke up, her voice shaking slightly as she began to share her struggles. "I've been feeling really overwhelmed lately. I worry that I'm not enough," she confessed. As she spoke, she noticed her family's expressions shift from lightheartedness to concern. They looked at her with warmth, ready to listen.

When Sophie finished, there was a moment of silence. She feared that her admission would change how they viewed her. Would they see her as weak? But instead of judgment, Sophie felt an enveloping embrace of support that surprised her. Her mother was the first to respond, expressing gratitude that Sophie had chosen to share her feelings. She shared her own experiences with insecurity, revealing that even as an adult, she often felt unprepared for the challenges of life.

Sophie realized then that her mother had also faced her battles. This was a defining moment, as it showed her that everyone, regardless of age or experience, could feel vulnerable. She learned that sharing her feelings fostered understanding and emotional connection. Instead of a silence filled with judgment, there was a bond forming, built on shared experiences and mutual support.

Sophie's father chimed in with his thoughts, recounting a time when he had felt inadequate in his career. He admitted that he had struggled with his confidence during a big project and had worried about letting everyone down. By revealing these worries, he found that he was not alone. His colleagues supported him, and together they managed to overcome their challenges. This shared story made Sophie realize that vulnerability could lead to teamwork and collaboration.

Her brother, usually the protector, opened up as well. He shared how he often felt pressure to be a perfect student and athlete. It was a relief for him to express these feelings, as he did not want to let his peers or family down. The weight of high expectations rested heavily on his shoulders. Hearing his sister share her emotions allowed him to feel comfortable admitting his own. Together, they found common ground in their vulnerabilities, discovering that the challenges they faced could actually strengthen their bonds.

As they continued to discuss their experiences, Sophie learned the importance of communication in relationships. Each story shared was like a thread weaving them closer together. The act of being open about their insecurities gave them all a sense of relief and solidarity. Instead of feeling alone in their struggles, they now felt a sense of community.

Sophie also reflected on how vulnerability relates to resilience. By sharing their struggles, they learned to cope with their emotions rather than bottle them up. Her family created a safe space where they could be honest without fear of ridicule. When one person expressed their worries, others were encouraged to join in, creating a chain reaction of openness. This collective honesty emboldened Sophie to face her own fears head-on.

She also considered how vulnerability was an essential part of growth. In revealing her struggles, she was taking steps toward self-acceptance. As she learned more about herself and how to navigate her feelings, she realized that vulnerability wasn't a sign of weakness, but a demonstration of courage. In fact, the act of opening up required immense strength.

Moved by the discussion, Sophie thought about actionable steps that could help not just her but the entire family. They agreed to set aside time each week to check in with each other. It would be a time where they could openly share what was on their minds, creating a space for valuable conversations. They decided that these gatherings would not only allow them to express their worries, but also to support one another as they worked through their challenges.

This initiative felt important to Sophie. She believed that other families could benefit from similar practices. Establishing a routine where everyone can share their feelings encourages emotional literacy and strengthens familial ties. It teaches the importance of being present for one another, recognizing when someone is having a difficult time.

Sophie's journey also made her think about the difference between vulnerability and oversharing. She realized that it was important to discern the right time and place for disclosures. While being open is valuable, people also need to be mindful of their audience and context. Sharing should foster connection, not overwhelm others with too much information at once.

Listening became another key topic of discussion among them. Sophie's family emphasized how crucial it is to not only speak about feelings but also to listen intently. To truly hear one another, they needed to offer their full attention and empathy. Active listening fosters an environment where everyone feels valued and respected.

Sophie's vulnerability led to a transformation in the family dynamic. They made a conscious effort to practice gratitude and appreciation. They learned to celebrate each other's strengths while being supportive during tough times. This created a balance where everyone felt uplifted rather than judged.

As days turned into weeks, Sophie noticed changes in herself. She began to embrace her insecurities instead of fearing them. By sharing her worries, she felt empowered, even discovering new coping mechanisms through family advice and shared experiences. She felt more confident in herself, realizing that vulnerability was not about weakness but actually about embracing her true self.

Through her journey, Sophie discovered that everyone struggles with their emotions at some point. By daring to be vulnerable, she learned to forge deeper connections. The conversations that flowed through her family helped lay the groundwork for stronger relationships. With every story shared, they became stronger together, allowing each person to find strength in their vulnerability.

As the chapter unfolded, Sophie felt grateful for the experiences gained through opening up. Embracing vulnerability allowed her to break down barriers that had long held her back. Each moment spent in honest conversation brought comfort and clarity, reinforcing the lesson that vulnerability is a source of strength, capable of uniting hearts and forging lasting relationships.

Sophie has always understood the importance of having people around her, but now she truly realizes how crucial a supportive network is in her life. Supportive people can make a significant difference during tough times, helping her navigate challenges and celebrate successes. To build this network, Sophie decides to focus on her relationships with family, friends, and teachers. This is a deliberate choice that will benefit her in various ways.

Starting with her family, Sophie recognizes that they have always been there for her. They provide a foundation of love and understanding. To strengthen these ties, Sophie makes an effort to spend more time with them. She initiates family dinners on weekends, where everyone comes together to eat and talk. Sharing meals encourages open communication, allowing her to express her feelings and listen to their experiences too. Sophie realizes that these gatherings foster a sense of belonging and make her feel secure. She also discovers that sharing personal stories creates deeper connections.

Friends play a crucial role in Sophie's support network as well. She reflects on her friendships and notices that some friends have drifted away. To remedy this, she reaches out to reconnect. Sophie sends texts to old friends, suggesting they meet for coffee or lunch. During these get-togethers, she listens actively and shares her own updates. She finds that reconnecting with old friends brings back cherished memories while also creating new ones. Through these commitments, Sophie learns to nurture her friendships. She plans to be more present and available for her friends, whether it's through regular chats or unexpected outings.

In addition to family and friends, Sophie understands the importance of her teachers in her support network. Teachers can be invaluable guides in both academic and personal matters. To strengthen her relationship with her teachers, she decides to communicate more openly with them. Sophie starts attending office hours, where she asks questions about her studies and seeks advice on her future. These interactions help her gain clarity and confidence in her decisions. Moreover, Sophie notices that her teachers appreciate her initiative and willingness to learn. This fosters a positive atmosphere where teachers are more willing to support her.

Sophie also considers joining clubs or groups that interest her. Being part of a community can add a new dimension to her support network. She explores different options, like a book club or a sports team, which can help her meet new people who share her interests. By participating in these activities, Sophie finds common ground with others and builds friendships based on shared experiences. She learns the importance of teamwork and collaboration through these interactions.

While building her support network, Sophie acknowledges that it takes time and effort. She adopts a proactive approach by reaching out to people and regularly checking in on them. Sophie starts by setting simple goals. For instance, she aims to message her friends every week, encouraging them to share what's happening in their lives. As she continues this practice, Sophie finds that her friends respond positively, leading to rekindled friendships. It also opens up opportunities for deeper conversations about their dreams and concerns.

Sophie realizes that being supportive is a two-way street. She wants to be there for her loved ones just as they are there for her. When someone calls needing to vent or ask for help, Sophie makes it a point to listen attentively without interrupting. She offers her thoughts or advice only when they seek it. This practice deepens her relationships and nurtures a sense of trust within her support network. When her friends see Sophie as a dependable person, they are more likely to confide in her.

Setting boundaries is another important aspect of building a support network. Sophie learns that while it is essential to be available for her friends and family, she must also prioritize her own needs. She reflects on her commitments and evaluates what might be overwhelming her. By understanding her limits, Sophie can engage with her support network fully without burning out. She communicates her boundaries when necessary, ensuring her relationships remain healthy and respectful.

In times of stress, Sophie turns to her support network for comfort. She finds that sharing her concerns with trusted individuals helps alleviate her worries. When facing academic pressures, Sophie discusses her struggles with her family, who provide encouragement and advice. At the same time, talking to friends allows her to share experiences and learn how others cope with similar stressors.

The act of giving and receiving support strengthens Sophie's connections. As she offers her help to others, she notices a positive feedback loop. Supporting her friends during their tough times brings her joy and reinforces their bond. For example, when a friend is going through a breakup, Sophie takes the initiative to plan activities that lift her friend's spirits. They enjoy time at the movies, going for hikes, or simply hanging out at home. Sophie sees how being there for others makes her feel more connected and reinforces her commitment to her support network.

As Sophie continues to build her support network, she also embraces vulnerability. She learns that sharing personal struggles can be a powerful way to deepen relationships. During discussions with friends, she opens up about her insecurities and fears, allowing them to do the same. This exchange of vulnerability fosters empathy and compassion. Sophie feels a sense of relief knowing that she is not alone in her challenges. It creates space for mutual support, where everyone can rely on one another during difficult times.

Sophie knows that maintaining a support network requires ongoing effort. She makes a conscious decision to keep nurturing her relationships. This involves celebrating her friends' successes and being present in their lives. Whether it's attending their events or simply sending a congratulatory message, Sophie recognizes the importance of showing her support. By doing this, she further solidifies her place in their lives and strengthens the bond that they share.

Engaging with her support network also helps Sophie develop essential social skills. She becomes more adept at communicating her thoughts and feelings effectively. By practicing active listening, she learns to pay attention to non-verbal cues and understand unspoken emotions. These skills serve her well in building relationships both socially and academically.

In addition to personal growth, Sophie realizes that her support network benefits her emotional well-being. She feels more confident knowing she can rely on those around her. In moments of uncertainty, having trustworthy people to confide in provides reassurance. This emotional safety net encourages her to take risks and pursue her goals.

As time goes on, Sophie's efforts to build her support network pay off in impactful ways. She finds comfort in knowing she is surrounded by a diverse group of supporters, each offering unique perspectives and experiences. This enhances her understanding of the world, broadening her horizons and enriching her life.

Chapter 18: Embracing Spirituality

Sophie sat quietly in her grandmother's garden, surrounded by vibrant flowers and the gentle hum of nature. The afternoon sun bathed the space in warm light, creating a serene atmosphere. It was here that her grandmother began to speak about spirituality. She explained that spirituality is about connecting to something larger than ourselves. For Sophie, this was a new concept, one that sparked her curiosity. Her grandmother suggested that they explore different ways to achieve this connection, and Sophie listened intently.

The first suggestion was to immerse themselves in nature. Her grandmother shared stories of how spending time outdoors often led to deeper reflections and a sense of belonging. They decided to take long walks in the nearby woods. As they strolled, her grandmother pointed out various trees, plants, and wildlife. She explained how each element contributes to the ecosystem, highlighting the interconnectedness of life. Sophie began to understand that being in nature wasn't just about observing; it was about feeling a part of it all.

On one of their walks, they found a quiet spot near a stream. Here, they sat on a fallen log, listening to the water flow and the birds sing. Her grandmother encouraged Sophie to close her eyes and take deep breaths, inhaling the fresh scent of pine and earth. This simple act of being present in the moment helped Sophie feel a wave of calm wash over her. Her grandmother explained that this was a form of meditation, a way to clear the mind and connect with the world around them.

Sophie learned that meditation can take many forms. It doesn't always mean sitting still for long periods. Sometimes, it can be as simple as focusing fully on a task or moment. Her grandmother introduced her to mindfulness, a practice of being aware of thoughts and feelings without judgment. They practiced this by sharing a meal. Instead of engaging in conversation, they focused on the colors, textures, and flavors of the food. Sophie realized how often she rushed through meals without appreciating them. This new approach brought the food to life and deepened her enjoyment.

In addition to nature and meditation, her grandmother spoke about the power of quiet reflection. They created a cozy nook at home where Sophie could sit comfortably with a journal. Each evening, they would take a few moments to write down their thoughts and feelings. Her grandmother explained that writing could be a powerful way to connect with oneself. It allows people to process their emotions and articulate their experiences. Sophie found this practice liberating, as it helped her understand her feelings more clearly and provided an outlet for expression.

Sometimes, her grandmother suggested, it might be useful to read books or listen to talks on spirituality. They would spend evenings discussing various texts. Each book offered a new perspective on the meaning of life and the importance of connecting with a greater purpose. They read about various beliefs, traditions, and practices. This not only broadened Sophie's understanding but also deepened her curiosity about the world around her. It became apparent to her that spirituality was not confined to one definition or practice but was a personal journey.

Sophie's grandmother also introduced her to the idea of service. She explained that helping others can enhance one's spiritual life. They volunteered at a local food bank, where they sorted donations and prepared meals. Through these experiences, Sophie witnessed firsthand the impact that kindness and compassion can have. She saw how her actions, no matter how small, could contribute to a larger purpose. It felt fulfilling to be part of something meaningful, and she realized that connecting to others was another way to embrace spirituality.

As they delved deeper, her grandmother shared the importance of asking questions. Spirituality often revolves around the big questions in life: Who are we? Why are we here? What connects us? Sophie learned that it was okay not to have all the answers. In fact, the process of seeking understanding could be just as important. They would sit together, pondering these questions and exploring their meanings. Through this contemplative practice, Sophie began to appreciate the beauty of exploration, knowing that it was a journey rather than a destination.

Sophie's grandmother encouraged her to create rituals that felt meaningful. They started small by lighting a candle each evening and taking a moment to reflect on their day. This simple act became a cherished part of their routine. It allowed them to pause and consider what they were grateful for. Gratitude, her grandmother said, is a powerful way to connect to the present moment and to acknowledge the good in life. Sophie began to notice the little things she might have previously overlooked—the warmth of her grandmother's smile, the laughter they shared, the beauty of a sunset.

They also explored the concept of community. Her grandmother emphasized that while individual practices are important, spirituality can thrive in community settings. They attended local gatherings and discussions, where people shared their stories and experiences. Sophie found herself inspired by the diverse perspectives others offered. Each story had its own lessons and resonated with her in different ways. She learned that being part of a community can foster connection and understanding, strengthening her spiritual journey.

Throughout their exploration, Sophie realized that embracing spirituality was not about rigid beliefs or strict practices. It was about being open to experiences and finding what resonated with her. Whether through nature, meditation, service, or community, Sophie discovered various paths to connect with something greater. Each step along the journey contributed to her growth and understanding.

As this chapter of her life unfolded, Sophie understood that spirituality is a personal journey, one that evolves over time. With her grandmother's guidance, she felt empowered to continue exploring her beliefs and practices. There was a sense of excitement in the unknown, knowing that the journey was just beginning. Every moment, every encounter, and every thought could enrich her understanding of herself and the world around her. With a heart full of gratitude, Sophie looked forward to what lay ahead, eager to embrace all that life had to offer.

Chapter 19: Journaling Your Journey

Sophie recently decided to start a journal. This choice was not made lightly; it came after many moments of reflection about her own life. The act of putting pen to paper felt like an inviting opportunity for her to explore her thoughts and feelings. Journaling became her personal sanctuary, a unique space where she could articulate her experiences in a clear manner. Every time she opened her notebook, she found herself in a comforting environment that welcomed her true self.

At first, Sophie struggled with what to write. The blank pages seemed daunting. She wondered if her thoughts were interesting enough or if she would be judged later. To ease this tension, she began with simple prompts. These prompts could be as straightforward as "What made me smile today?" or "What challenges did I face this week?" By using these guiding questions, Sophie found a pathway into her emotions. This practice opened the door to deeper reflections, encouraging her to write freely without the fear of judgment.

As Sophie continued her journaling journey, she noticed how it helped her process her emotions. When she faced days filled with joy, anger, or sadness, she would write about those feelings. For instance, on a day when she felt overwhelmed by stress at work, she described her worries about meeting deadlines. By writing it all down, those overwhelming emotions felt lighter. It was as if the heavy load began to lift, leaving her with clearer thoughts. She found it helpful to dissect her feelings, examining what triggered her anxiety and how she might manage it better in the future.

Sophie also found comfort in reflecting on her personal growth through journaling. As she wrote regularly, she realized how much she had changed over time. She could look back at her entries to see how her thoughts and feelings evolved. For example, early in her journaling days, Sophie often wrote about self-doubt and insecurity. But as weeks turned into months, her entries began to mirror her increasing confidence. This evolution revealed an important truth: writing about her experiences allowed her to track her journey, and see that she was indeed making progress.

To keep her journaling engaging, Sophie experimented with various styles. Initially, she tried narrative storytelling, detailing events from her day-to-day life. Later on, she transitioned to lists, noting what she was grateful for or outlining her dreams and goals. These lists not only inspired her but also became motivation to continue pursuing her aspirations. For example, she made a checklist of places she wanted to visit, which gave her a sense of direction and purpose. By taking these steps, Sophie noticed how her journaling became a multi-faceted tool for managing her life.

One day, Sophie decided to create a special section in her journal dedicated to gratitude. Each evening, she would jot down three things she appreciated that day. Sometimes it was something as simple as a warm cup of coffee or a friendly conversation with a coworker. Other times, it was about the bigger things, like the support of family or the opportunity to learn something new. By focusing on gratitude, Sophie shifted her mindset. Instead of ruminating on negative experiences, she learned to find joy in the small moments. This practice became a source of joy and ease in her daily routine.

Sophie also began reflecting on her writing itself. Occasionally, she would look back at her earlier entries and analyze her growth not only as a person but as a writer. This reflection allowed her to identify recurring themes in her thoughts. For instance, she noticed that many of her challenges were linked to her fear of failure. Recognizing this pattern enabled her to consciously work on her fears, rather than letting them dictate her decisions. With each page, she grew more empowered, understanding that her voice mattered and that her feelings deserved to be expressed openly.

As her journal evolved, Sophie became more adventurous in her writing. She experimented with different formats, such as poetry and letters. Writing poetry allowed her to express complex emotions in a simple way. Letters, especially those meant for her future self, provided a mechanism for accountability. In a letter she wrote to herself a year from then, she described her hopes and dreams, urging her future self to remain committed to her path. This exercise in foresight instilled a sense of purpose and connection to her journey.

Journaling also became a catalyst for Sophie to document her experiences with others. She began including stories about her friends and family, celebrating moments of laughter and connection within her entries. These anecdotes not only enriched her writing but also reminded her of the support system surrounding her. For instance, she wrote about an inspiring conversation with a friend discussing their dreams, which motivated Sophie to pursue her own ambitions with renewed vigor. By capturing these moments, she cultivated a sense of community within the pages of her journal.

Moreover, Sophie explored the benefits of reviewing her journaling practice periodically. She set aside time each month to reflect on her entries. This review process granted her a comprehensive view of her journey. By summarizing her thoughts and feelings from the past weeks, she identified patterns and themes. This self-assessment enabled her to celebrate victories, no matter how small, and

identify areas where she wanted to grow
further. It became a rewarding and
enlightening ritual, shedding light on her
progress.

Sophie also viewed journaling as a
means of self-care. On challenging days,
she created a cozy ambiance for her
writing. This included lighting a candle,
sipping herbal tea, and playing soft music
in the background. By doing so, she
transformed the journaling experience
into a comforting routine. It served not
only as a source of reflection but also as
a way to unwind from her daily stresses.
This mindful approach to journaling
emphasized the importance of taking
time for herself amid her busy schedule.

Through her journaling journey, Sophie
eventually came to regard her journal as
more than just a collection of thoughts. It
transformed into a cherished companion

that witnessed her struggles, victories, and everything in between. Each entry was a testament to her growth, marking the path she walked. As she flipped through the pages, she felt proud of the journey she had undertaken. Journaling had become a powerful tool, providing clarity, self-awareness, and tangible proof of her progress.

Chapter 20: Handling Social Media Stress

Sophie sat on her couch, scrolling through her phone as images filled her screen. Bright photos of friends having fun, perfect vacations, and glamorous lifestyles surrounded her. However, instead of feeling happy, she felt a growing sense of unease. Each image seemed to amplify her own insecurities and anxiety. Sophie began to realize that what she saw was not a true representation of real life. She often caught herself comparing her behind-the-scenes moments to the highlights that others seemed to share without hesitation. This realization brought about thoughts of the pressure that social media placed on both her and others.

Sophie decided to dive deeper into her feelings. Was she the only one feeling this way? A quick chat with her friends revealed that they too found themselves under stress because of social media. They often felt the need to appear perfect online, which led to feelings of inadequacy and anxiety when reality did not match up. The constant notifications, likes, and comments created an environment where people felt they had to perform. Sophie and her friends recognized that this wasn't just about them; it was a broader issue affecting many people in their lives.

After reflecting on her experiences and those of her friends, Sophie recognized that taking a break from social media might help her regain perspective. She set a specific timeline for her break, deciding to step away for one month. During this month, she planned to focus more on her real-life connections and experiences instead of virtual interactions. Making this choice was empowering. Sophie felt a sense of control as she considered the positive changes she could make in her life without the constant presence of social media.

To make her break easier, Sophie took some practical steps. First, she deleted the apps from her phone to reduce the temptation to check them. As simple as it sounded, this action helped her break the cycle of constant scrolling. Though she found herself reaching for her phone out of habit, each time she remembered her decision to take a break, she felt a sense of pride. Instead of scrolling through posts, she redirected her energy toward activities that brought her joy.

Sophie started by reconnecting with her hobbies. She had loved painting as a child but had not picked up a brush in years. Remembering the joy it brought her, she set up a small painting station in her living room. As she painted, she found joy in expressing herself creatively, a feeling she had missed while scrolling through her feed. Each stroke of the brush felt like a breath of fresh air, reminding her of the importance of nurturing her passions and interests.

In addition to painting, Sophie also began to spend more quality time with her friends and family. She organized game nights and movie marathons, where laughter and conversation replaced the endless cycle of likes and comments. These gatherings created a deeper bond with her loved ones. She saw that real-life interactions brought warmth and joy that social media simply could not replicate. Each interaction felt genuine, bringing a smile to her face that no number of likes could ever match.

Understanding the impact of social media on mental health also led Sophie to seek knowledge about managing online stress. She immersed herself in books and articles about the psychological effects of social media. Sophie learned about the phenomenon of FOMO, or "fear of missing out," and how it created feelings of insecurity and anxiety. She realized that many people, including herself, felt left out when they saw others enjoying experiences that seemed unattainable. This awareness helped her appreciate her own unique experiences, seeing them as valuable and fulfilling in their own right.

Sophie also began practicing mindfulness. She learned to focus on the present moment, taking time each day to breathe, meditate, or just reflect. Mindfulness became a powerful tool in handling her stress. It taught her to recognize when she was slipping back into negative thoughts about social media. Whenever she felt the urge to check her phone, she paused and took a moment to breathe deeply instead. This simple practice helped calm her anxiety and clear her thoughts, allowing her to focus on what truly mattered.

As days turned into weeks, Sophie noticed a positive transformation within herself. The pressures she once felt from social media began to fade. She became more confident in herself and less concerned about how others perceived her. Through her journey, she found that it was important to define her self-worth outside of social media metrics. The number of likes, followers, or comments no longer dictated her mood; she focused on meaningful relationships, personal growth, and self-acceptance.

When Sophie did return to social media after her month-long break, she approached it with a new mindset. She unfollowed accounts that made her feel inadequate and instead focused on those that inspired her. This included pages dedicated to art, wellness, and positive mental health. Curating her social media feed allowed her to create a more uplifting online experience, one that aligned with her values and interests.

Sophie also made it a point to post more authentically. Rather than sharing only her highlight reel, she started to include moments that showed the real, raw, and sometimes messy sides of life. She reflected on the importance of vulnerability and connection. By being open about her struggles, she not only felt freer but also helped others feel less alone in their own journeys.

Through her experience, Sophie learned that it was okay to take breaks, prioritize mental health, and focus on what truly mattered in life. Social media could be used positively, but it required mindfulness and intentionality. By fostering real connections and engaging in activities that brought joy, Sophie discovered a balance that allowed her to thrive both online and offline. Her journey had just begun, but she felt equipped to navigate the world of social media in a way that honored her well-being and true self.

Chapter 21: Helping Others

Sophie begins to notice that some of her friends are going through tough times. These struggles are not always obvious at first. Sometimes, friends may seem fine on the surface, but a closer look reveals signs of sadness, anxiety, or stress. For example, Sophie observes that her friend, Emma, who usually loves to laugh and chat, has become quieter lately. Emma often seems lost in thought or distracted, missing out on activities they used to enjoy together. This change in Emma prompts Sophie to think carefully about how important it is to be aware of the emotions and struggles of those around her.

As Sophie reflects on her friendships, she realizes that many people face challenges in their lives. It might be stress from school, problems at home, or feelings of loneliness. Sophie understands that when we help others, it can create a sense of connection that is beneficial for both parties. When she approaches Emma with kindness and concern, Sophie begins to understand that the simple act of reaching out can lighten the burden her friend carries. Sophie asks Emma if she would like to talk about what's bothering her, showing that she is there to listen. This invitation can be a significant step, as it opens the door for deeper conversations.

Helping others doesn't require grand gestures. It can be as simple as sending a text to check on someone, inviting them to join an activity, or just being present. Sophie decides to invite Emma to a cozy movie night at her house. This small act not only provides Emma with an opportunity to share her feelings but also allows Sophie to show her support in a comfortable setting. By doing this, Sophie discovers that providing support can strengthen their bond and allows her to feel more connected.

In addition to Emma, Sophie notices that her other friends, like Jake and Mia, also seem to be struggling. She decides to reach out to them as well. Sophie learns that Jake has been feeling overwhelmed with schoolwork, and Mia is dealing with some family issues. Rather than pushing them to talk about their problems if they are not ready, Sophie uses a gentle approach. She encourages open conversations but allows her friends to share only if they feel comfortable. This way, Sophie respects their boundaries while still being available for help.

One effective way Sophie realizes she can help her friends is by organizing group activities. She plans a fun day at the park where everyone can come together, breathe fresh air, and simply enjoy each other's company. This setting creates a relaxed atmosphere where her friends can feel at ease to talk, laugh, and enjoy themselves. This simple gathering helps to break the ice. It creates a space for them to open up, share experiences, and support one another. Sophie sees the positive impact of these gatherings as laughter fills the air and smiles return to their faces.

Learning to help others also benefits Sophie's mental health. She feels a sense of purpose and fulfillment when she can support her friends. It brings her joy to see them smile and feel less alone in their struggles. This realization deepens her understanding of kindness and empathy. Sophie understands that while she is providing help, she, in turn, is also nurturing her own emotional well-being. Research shows that helping others can lead to increased happiness and satisfaction in one's life, which becomes evident to her.

Sophie also begins to learn new skills that are important when helping others.

For instance, active listening becomes a key focus. This means giving full attention and responding with understanding. When Emma shares her worries, Sophie practices reflecting back what her friend says, summarizing her feelings, and validating her emotions. This shows Emma that her feelings are important and that she is genuinely cared for. This approach positions Sophie as a safe space for her friends, where they can express their worries without fear of being judged.

Sophie also realizes the importance of encouraging her friends to seek professional help if needed. She understands that while friends can support each other, there are times when speaking to a counselor or therapist is really crucial. She researches local resources and discusses this with her friends. For example, she mentions a school counselor who specializes in helping students cope with stress. By doing this, Sophie empowers her friends to take the next step if they feel overwhelmed and need extra support.

In her journey of helping others, Sophie learns to recognize the signs when a friend is not doing well. She understands the importance of checking in more often. Instead of waiting for someone to reach out, she starts sending texts regularly, asking how they are doing. She seeks to be more proactive in offering help, showing her willingness to be there without making her friends feel pressured. This habit builds trust and encourages her friends to reach out to her when they need someone to talk to.

Furthermore, Sophie finds that it's essential to take care of herself while helping others. She learns about self-care and the importance of setting boundaries. This means knowing when to take a step back and recharge her own energy. For instance, after spending a long weekend helping friends, Sophie takes a day for herself to relax and enjoy activities that make her happy. She reads a book, goes for a walk, or spends time on her hobbies. By doing this, she realizes that being strong for others requires her to be in a good place herself.

Sophie's experiences lead her to understand the long-term effects of kindness and support in friendships. Over time, these small actions of kindness create a ripple effect. Her friends begin to help each other, forming a supportive community. Sophie notices that Emma, Jake, and Mia also start checking in on their friends, continuing the cycle of kindness. This new dynamic not only brings the group closer but also creates an environment where everyone feels safe to express their feelings.

In addition to her friends, Sophie starts to extend her kindness to those outside her immediate circle. She begins volunteering at a local community center where she can help others in various ways. Whether it's tutoring younger kids, cleaning up local parks, or just offering companionship to the elderly, Sophie finds fulfillment in giving back. This experience teaches her that kindness can take many forms and reach a broader audience.

Through her journey of helping others, Sophie learns there is an art to kindness, one that requires practice, patience, and an open heart. She becomes more aware of the importance of connection and the simple yet profound impact of caring for those around her. As she navigates through her friendships, she gathers countless memories filled with laughter, tears, and shared experiences. These moments define the essence of love and compassion, not just within her circle of friends but as a way of life.

Chapter 22: Dealing with Grief

Sophie recently lost her beloved pet, a small dog named Max. This was a significant event in her young life, as it was the first time she faced the pain of losing someone she loved. Max was not just a pet; he was her companion, sleeping by her side and keeping her company during tough times. Losing him created a deep, aching void in her heart. Sophie felt an overwhelming sadness that she had never experienced before. The initial shock made it hard for her to comprehend the reality of the situation.

Her family noticed Sophie's struggles with her feelings. They gathered around her to provide support and comfort. Sophie's parents explained that grief is a natural response to loss. They shared their own experiences of losing loved ones, which helped Sophie understand that she was not alone. They emphasized that many people go through grief and that it is an important part of life. It can be difficult, but it is also normal. With each shared story, Sophie began to feel understood.

As days passed, Sophie found herself caught in a whirlwind of emotions. Some days, she would feel okay, able to play with her toys or watch her favorite shows. Other days, she felt like crying for hours. Her parents encouraged her to express her feelings. They suggested she could talk to them about her emotions or write them down in a journal. Writing became a helpful outlet for Sophie. Each time she put her thoughts on paper, it felt like a small release from the heavy load she was carrying.

One evening, Sophie sat down with her journal. She wrote about the special moments she shared with Max. She recalled their long walks in the park, where he would chase after squirrels and bark playfully. Sophie wrote about how Max would sit by her feet while she did her homework, always there to encourage her. Remembering the happy times made her smile even amid the pain. This exercise taught her that cherishing memories could help ease her heartache.

Sophie's family also helped her create a memorial for Max. They chose a small spot in the garden, where Sophie could visit and remember her pet. Together, they planted flowers and made a small wooden sign with Max's name on it. This act helped Sophie feel connected to Max, even after his passing. It was a beautiful way to honor him and keep his memory alive. Each time she watered the flowers, she felt like she was expressing her love for him.

Understanding grief means recognizing that it does not have a set timeline. Sophie learned that healing takes time, and it is okay to feel sadness long after the loss. Her family reminded her that some days would be harder than others, and that was perfectly normal. They encouraged Sophie to take her time in healing and not rush through her feelings. Some days, the weight of her grief felt heavy, while on others, she could find moments of joy.

Sophie also found comfort in talking about Max with her friends. They shared stories of pets they had lost, and in doing so, she realized that they understood her pain. Together they created a space where they could be open about their feelings. This connection helped Sophie realize that others were also grappling with loss, and speaking about it brought them closer.

In addition to sharing stories, Sophie's family introduced her to various activities that could help ease her grief. They suggested drawing. Art became another way for Sophie to express herself. She created vibrant pictures of Max, capturing his bright eyes and playful spirit. Each stroke of color on the paper was a form of healing. It was a way to celebrate Max's life while helping Sophie process her own feelings.

Through these activities, Sophie began to understand that grief could transform. It started as a deep sadness but slowly evolved into a loving remembrance of Max. As time went by, she noticed that the intensity of her grief lessened. Although she missed Max dearly, she could also smile when thinking of him. There were moments of joy amid her sadness. She learned that it was not necessary to feel guilty for being happy about other moments in life.

Sophie's parents continued to educate her about grief and loss. They explained that everyone handles grief differently. Some people keep busy, while others may prefer solitude. Some individuals find solace in discussions, while others may process their feelings quietly. Sophie recognized this diversity and learned to respect how others managed their grief. This awareness fostered empathy in her, as she could support friends and family members when they encountered loss.

During one family gathering, Sophie's grandparents shared stories from their own lives. They spoke about the pets they had lost, the friends who had moved away, and how they learned to carry those memories with them. Sophie's heart swelled with pride to hear her family's resilience. Their stories made her realize that loss is a universal experience, and it connects people even more deeply. In sharing those memories, Sophie saw that time could help heal wounds, making room for hope and new experiences.

Sophie decided to honor Max in her own special way. She thought about how much joy he brought her and how she wanted to bring joy to others too. Inspired, she began volunteering at an animal shelter. This experience allowed her to help other animals looking for homes while reflecting on Max's spirit. Each puppy and kitten she met became a tiny piece of her healing journey. Helping these animals filled her heart with warmth and love, giving her purpose beyond her pain.

As Sophie continued her journey through grief, she learned that it is important to remember the lessons that loss teaches. She discovered the value of life, the strength of memories, and the importance of compassion. Grief may come without warning, but it can lead to a deeper understanding of what we cherish the most. Sophie understood that grief is a part of love. It means we have loved deeply and that those we love will always have a special place in our hearts.

Through the guidance of her family and the loving memories of Max, Sophie embraced her feelings. She learned to accept her grief while cherishing the love that will always remain in her heart. Each step in her journey brought her closer to healing and helped her appreciate the time they spent together. Sophie's experience taught her that while loss is painful, it can also illuminate the strength of love and connection, even in difficult times.

Chapter 23: Finding Balance

Sophie was always on the go. She had school, hobbies, and friends pulling her in different directions. At first, she enjoyed being busy. Each day was filled with activities, and she felt productive and accomplished. However, as time went on, she began to feel overwhelmed. The pressure of keeping up with her responsibilities became heavy. She noticed that her energy levels were dropping, and she often felt stressed. Something needed to change.

To regain control, Sophie decided it was time to find a balance in her life. She realized that balancing her schedule was not just about managing her time. It was also about understanding her priorities and recognizing what truly mattered to her. At this point, she began to think about how she could reorganize her life in a way that allowed her to enjoy her activities without feeling stretched too thin.

Sophie started by writing down everything she had on her plate. She made a list of all her classes, homework assignments, extracurricular activities, and social commitments. Seeing everything laid out in front of her helped Sophie assess how much she was really handling. It was eye-opening and slightly overwhelming. Some days, her schedule was packed from morning until night. This realization prompted her to make some changes.

Next, Sophie focused on identifying her priorities. She asked herself what activities brought her joy and fulfillment. Did she enjoy her dance class more than her science club? Was spending time with her friends more important than keeping up with some of her hobbies? With these questions in mind, she started to categorize her commitments into three groups: high priority, medium priority, and low priority.

High-priority activities were those that contributed to her goals or made her genuinely happy. For example, she decided that her dance class and spending time with friends were high priorities because they brought her joy and allowed her to express herself. On the other hand, some activities that she felt obligated to do, such as attending every meeting of the science club, fell into the low-priority category. This clarity helped Sophie understand where she could make adjustments.

With her priorities clear, Sophie created a new schedule. She started using a planner to map out her week. She allocated specific time slots for each of her high-priority activities. She gave herself ample time to complete homework and study, ensuring she was not cramming things at the last minute. This planning also included time for relaxation, something she often neglected. Sophie made a conscious effort to block out at least thirty minutes each day for herself, whether that was to read, take a walk, or just enjoy some peace and quiet.

Sophie's new schedule was not without its challenges. There were still days when unexpected events would pop up, changing her plans. A last-minute group study session or a friend wanting to hang out could disrupt her carefully laid plans. At first, this frustrated her. However, she learned to be flexible. If something important came up, she would adapt her schedule rather than feel defeated. This ability to adjust was a key part of finding balance.

As Sophie continued to practice her new routine, she found that her stress levels decreased. By committing to her high-priority activities and allowing herself flexibility, she felt more in control. She also started to notice that she enjoyed her classes and hobbies more now that she wasn't constantly worrying about fitting everything in.

There was another benefit to finding balance in her life. Sophie began discovering new interests and passions. With her structured schedule, she started exploring different activities that she had previously put on the back burner. She joined a book club that met once a week, which not only provided her with new friendships but also encouraged her love for reading. It was enriching to her life without overwhelming her.

Sophie also made a point to check in with herself regularly. Every couple of weeks, she would review her schedule to see if it still felt right. This practice was essential for maintaining balance. She recognized that her interests and responsibilities could change over time, so staying mindful of her feelings helped her continue evolving her routine.

Additionally, Sophie started to communicate with her friends about her need for balance. She explained that, while she loved spending time with them, there would be times she might not be able to hang out as often. Her friends were understanding and supportive. They began to coordinate their schedules too, ensuring they could still enjoy time together without making her feel stretched thin.

Sophie also learned about the importance of setting boundaries. At times, she felt guilty for saying no to requests or invitations. However, imposing limits on how much she could take on was key to maintaining her mental health. By explaining her reasoning to her friends, she was able to uphold her boundaries while still keeping her relationships strong. Setting boundaries meant she could prioritize her commitments effectively.

There were moments when Sophie experienced setbacks — days when she felt overwhelmed despite her best efforts. During those times, she would reflect on her goals and values. Understanding that finding balance was a journey made those setbacks easier to handle. Instead of getting discouraged, she viewed them as opportunities to learn more about herself and her needs.

In addition to her ongoing practice of balance, Sophie began to notice the value of self-care. She learned that taking care of herself physically and mentally was vital for maintaining balance. She made sure to get enough sleep, eat healthy meals, and stay active. Exercise became a crucial part of her routine, helping to reduce stress and improve her mood. Recognizing the signs of exhaustion early on allowed her to pause and rest when necessary.

Sophie also explored mindfulness as a way to find inner peace. Even just a few minutes of deep breathing or meditation helped her when she felt anxious. By practicing mindfulness, Sophie became more aware of her thoughts and feelings. This awareness allowed her to address issues before they spiraled into something overwhelming.

Through this journey of finding balance, Sophie learned that it was okay to ask for help. Whether it was reaching out to family for support or seeking guidance from teachers, she understood that everyone needs a little help sometimes. Her willingness to reach out strengthened her relationships and created a support system that helped her through tough times.

Finding balance was not just a one-time fix for Sophie. It was a continuous journey that required attention and adjustment. With time and effort, she found a rhythm that worked for her. She learned valuable lessons about prioritization, flexibility, and self-care — lessons that would continue to guide her in life. Sophie was not just busy anymore; she was engaged and fulfilled.

Chapter 24: The Journey Continues

Sophie sits in a quiet corner of her favorite café, a warm cup of herbal tea in her hands. As she takes a deep breath, she starts to think back to all the things she has learned about mental and spiritual health over recent months. Each lesson has shaped her in ways she never expected. She understands that taking care of the mind and soul is not a one-time task but an ongoing journey that requires patience, effort, and care. This realization feels empowering, as if she has finally grasped the importance of this journey.

To begin this journey, Sophie acknowledges the importance of mental health. She reflects on her past struggles, recalling times when stress felt overwhelming, and anxiety clouded her thoughts. She remembers the nights of tossing and turning, mind racing as her worries took center stage. Recognizing these feelings was the first step towards growth. Mental health is about understanding one's emotions, thoughts, and behaviors and how they influence each other. For Sophie, the journey started with mindfulness practices, which she discovered helped her gain awareness of her feelings without judgment.

Sophie found that mindful activities, such as meditation and journaling, allowed her to dissect her thoughts. Meditation taught her how to sit with her feelings and observe them like passing clouds. Writing in her journal provided her with a space to express herself freely, laying bare the trials and triumphs of her mind. These practices have not only enhanced her awareness but have also equipped her with tools to cope during turbulent times. She can see how expressing her feelings through writing helps her process emotions, and she realizes that many people might benefit from similar practices.

Beyond just understanding her mind, Sophie recognizes the value of engaging with her spiritual health. For her, spirituality is about connection, both with herself and the world around her. This year, she embarked on a journey to explore various spiritual practices, seeking what resonated with her. She started attending yoga classes, where the combination of movement and breath opened her to a new way of understanding her body. Each pose brought her closer to her inner self and made her appreciate the present moment. Sophie realizes that spirituality can take many forms, from yoga to nature walks, and it is about finding practices that touch her soul.

Sophie also explored the healing power of nature. She took walks in the park, enjoying the fresh air and the sounds of birds singing. Nature provided her a space to rejuvenate her spirit, allowing her to connect with the earth and appreciate its beauty. She learned to notice the small details around her—the colors of the leaves, the feel of the wind, and the sun warming her skin. These moments became vital reminders that life is happening all around her, inviting her to be present. She believes that spending time outdoors can inspire others to reconnect with their surroundings, providing a natural remedy for stress and anxiety.

During her journey, Sophie deepened her understanding of self-care. She discovered that self-care goes beyond bubble baths and pampering sessions; it involves treating oneself with kindness and respect. For Sophie, this meant setting healthy boundaries with her time and energy. She learned to say no without guilt when her plate was too full, which freed her up to focus on activities that truly invigorated her. By prioritizing self-care, she found she was more productive, happier, and better equipped to support others. She encourages anyone struggling with balance to explore what self-care means to them, emphasizing that it is a unique journey.

As Sophie reflects on her journey, she acknowledges the importance of seeking help when needed. There were moments when she felt overwhelmed and uncertain about her path. During these times, she reached out to friends and family. Their support reminded her that it's okay to ask for help. Talking with a therapist also played a significant role in her journey. It provided a safe space to unpack her feelings and gain new perspectives. Through therapy, she found clarity and tools to navigate her thoughts, which she now sees as crucial for her ongoing mental health.

From her experiences, Sophie wants to share actionable steps with anyone who may be starting their journey toward better mental and spiritual health. First, she suggests setting aside time each day to reflect. This could be through meditation, journaling, or simply sitting in silence. Creating a routine helps to embed these practices into daily life. Secondly, she emphasizes exploring different spiritual practices, such as yoga, tai chi, or even simple stretching. Each method offers its own unique benefits, and finding the right fit is essential.

Another practical step is to prioritize nature. Sophie encourages others to take short walks or plan weekend hikes, even if just to the local park. Immersing oneself in nature has profound effects; it lowers stress and lifts the spirit. Learning to appreciate these moments can transform one's outlook on life. She also advises making self-care a non-negotiable aspect of one's routine. This means scheduling downtime just as you would any important appointment.

Sophie believes it's vital to connect with a community or support network. Whether through online groups, local clubs, or friendships, sharing experiences creates bonds and reminds one they are not alone. This connection can provide encouragement and motivation, especially when faced with challenges. Lastly, she champions the idea of education. Reading books on mental and spiritual health, attending workshops, or listening to podcasts can enrich one's understanding and growth.

With a full heart, Sophie reflects on where her journey has led her. It has not always been easy, but she embraces the bumps along the road as part of her path. Each challenge provided a lesson, contributing to her growth. Now, she feels ready for whatever comes next in her life. Her journey is a continuous process, and she looks forward to each new discovery. Sophie knows that, while mental and spiritual health are ongoing pursuits, they are also sources of immense strength and peace. She accepts that there will always be more to learn and explore. This realization fuels her enthusiasm for the future.

Chapter 25: Sharing the Light

In this final chapter, we see Sophie take a significant step in her journey. After spending time learning about herself and the practices that promote a healthy mind and spirit, she feels compelled to share her knowledge with others. Sophie understands that the lessons she has learned about mindfulness, gratitude, and self-care are not just for her alone; they are meant to be shared. This realization gives her a sense of empowerment. She believes that by sharing these practices, she can help her friends and the wider community find peace and balance in their lives.

Sophie starts by gathering her close friends for a casual meetup. She wants to create a safe space where everyone feels comfortable to talk about their thoughts and emotions. In this gathering, she introduces the concept of mindfulness. Mindfulness means being present in the moment and fully engaging with whatever you are doing. For example, when eating, instead of rushing through a meal while scrolling on a phone, one can focus on the taste, texture, and aroma of the food. Sophie explains how this practice can help reduce stress and improve overall well-being.

As the conversation flows, Sophie encourages her friends to share their experiences. They discuss how stressful life can be and how easy it is to forget to take care of themselves. To illustrate how mindfulness can help, Sophie leads a simple mindfulness exercise. She asks everyone to close their eyes and focus on their breathing. Inhale deeply through the nose and exhale slowly through the mouth. This exercise lasts for a few minutes, and afterward, everyone feels a little more relaxed. Sophie expresses that taking just a few moments each day to practice mindfulness can make a big difference in how they handle stress.

Next, Sophie shifts the topic to gratitude. She explains the importance of recognizing the good things in life, no matter how small they may seem. Gratitude is about appreciating what you have instead of dwelling on what you lack. Sophie shares her own experience of keeping a gratitude journal. Every night, she writes down three things she is thankful for. This simple act has helped her stay positive, even during tough times. She encourages her friends to try writing in a gratitude journal as well. It doesn't have to be complicated; they can just jot down a few points each day.

Her friends express interest, but some mention they find it hard to notice the good in their lives. Sophie listens attentively and suggests they start small. She proposes that each of them can begin by acknowledging one good thing about their day before going to bed. It could be as simple as enjoying a delicious cup of coffee or having a pleasant chat with someone. By focusing on these positive moments, they can train their minds to look for more good in their daily lives.

Sophie also discusses self-care. She believes that taking care of oneself is crucial in maintaining mental and emotional health. Self-care can include many things, from physical activities like exercising or walking to enjoyable activities like reading or painting. Sophie shares her routine, which includes walking in the park while listening to her favorite music. This helps her clear her mind and rejuvenate. She encourages her friends to find their own self-care rituals that suit their personalities and lifestyle.

They talk about the challenges they face in making time for themselves. Sophie acknowledges that life can be busy and overwhelming. However, she emphasizes the importance of prioritizing self-care. She advises her friends to schedule "me time" into their calendars just like they would for work or other commitments. Making this time non-negotiable can help them stay connected to their own needs.

As the discussion deepens, Sophie invites her friends to share their own self-care ideas. They exchange thoughts on various activities that help them relax. Some of them suggest reading, while others enjoy cooking or spending time in nature. Sophie is thrilled to see them engaged and taking notes. She encourages them to try something new and to be open to exploring different activities. This sharing not only enhances their understanding but also fosters a sense of community.

Sophie feels a sense of fulfillment as she notices the positive energy in the room. She knows that the practices of mindfulness, gratitude, and self-care can transform lives. With this knowledge, she decides to take her journey a step further by planning a series of workshops. These workshops would allow her to reach more people in the community. Sophie envisions a space where individuals can come together to learn, practice, and share their experiences.

Over the next few weeks, Sophie dedicates time to organize the workshops. She creates a simple outline of topics to cover, including mindfulness techniques, ways to cultivate gratitude, and self-care tips. Sophie considers inviting local mental health professionals to join in and share their insights. This collaboration could offer participants a broader perspective and a more enriching experience.

She also thinks about the setting. A calm and inviting environment can make a big difference in how people feel during the workshops. Sophie decides to hold the sessions in the community center, where they have access to a garden. Being surrounded by nature can enhance the mindfulness practice they will explore.

Sophie believes it will create a peaceful atmosphere, allowing participants to connect with themselves and each other.

As the day of the first workshop arrives, Sophie is a mix of excited and nervous. She prepares the space by arranging chairs in a circle. This setup encourages openness and discussion. She sets out cozy cushions, soft lighting, and fresh flowers to create a warm ambiance. When participants arrive, they are greeted with smiles and light refreshments, helping them feel welcome and at ease.

Sophie begins the workshop by introducing herself and explaining her journey. She shares her experiences with mindfulness, gratitude, and self-care, just as she did with her friends. Participants listen attentively, nodding in understanding. Sophie guides them through a mindfulness exercise similar to the one she did with her friends. She notices a calming energy in the room, and everyone seems to appreciate the moment of tranquility.

Gradually, she introduces the concept of gratitude. Participants engage in a guided reflection where they identify things they are grateful for in their lives. Many individuals share their thoughts aloud, and this sharing builds a sense of community. They realize that many of them face similar challenges, and together, they can support each other on their journey to wellness.

Sophie wraps up the workshop by discussing self-care. She encourages participants to create a self-care plan tailored to their needs. Together, they brainstorm activities that bring them joy and relaxation. The room buzzes with ideas, laughter, and support. As the workshop comes to a close, Sophie feels fulfilled seeing her efforts make a difference. Participants leave with smiles and a renewed sense of hope and possibility.

In the following weeks, the workshops gain popularity. More individuals join, eager to learn from Sophie's insights. Each session builds upon the last, fostering a strong community of support. People share their progress in practicing mindfulness and gratitude, while others discuss how self-care has impacted their lives. Sophie feels grateful for the connections created through these gatherings.

Through this journey, Sophie realizes that sharing the light is a powerful tool. By encouraging others to explore mindfulness, gratitude, and self-care, she not only strengthens their lives but also her own. She knows that the light she shares will continue to grow as more people join in and practice these techniques. Sophie feels a deep sense of purpose and fulfillment in knowing that she is making a difference one person at a time.